# THE TECHNIQUE OF BUCKS POINT LACE

# THE TECHNIQUE
## OF
# BUCKS POINT LACE

Pamela Nottingham

Larousse and Co., Inc., *New York*

ISBN 0–88332–263–3

First published 1981 in the United States by Larousse & Co., Ltd., 572 Fifth Avenue, New York, New York 10036

Printed in Great Britain

# Contents

# FOREWORD

Two points of particular interest to lacemakers concern prickings and bobbins. Where do prickings come from and to whom do they belong? Original patterns are the property of the designer, but too often the contemporary designer remains unknown. I suggest that anyone who creates a new pattern signs the pricking close to the head or footside, and in this way will receive credit for his or her work.

However, most of our patterns are traditional. They have been preserved by lacemaking families, collectors or museums. In most cases, more than one so-called original copy exists and many more have been made.

It is no longer difficult to get lacemaking equipment; there are many stockists throughout the country. Whilst one can admire the old decorated bobbins and wonder at their inscriptions, it is good to know that the craft of bobbin making has been revived and that today there are people who choose to turn bobbins as a full time occupation. The contemporary bobbin maker does not ply his trade at village fairs as happened a century and more ago, but offers a mail order service and visits lace meetings. He, too, has accepted a challenge to make not only simple bobbins but also those which demonstrate true craftsmanship in the intricate use of wood, bone, wire and pewter.

# ACKNOWLEDGMENTS

I should like to thank Doreen Fudge, Keeper of Fine Arts at the Luton Museum and Art Gallery for her help and for access to the museum collection of lace, drafts and prickings. Also my thanks go to Miss S.E. Dawson of Speen who, over many years, has given to me old and fascinating patterns and shared her knowledge and enthusiasm.

I am grateful to Ann Cope, Beryl Maw, Audrey Norman, Joyce Symes and Pamela Tyrrell for permission to include photographs of their lace, also to Mr W. Bullock for the use of patterns and lace which belonged to his late wife, Freda. Patricia Philpott has kindly taken the photographs. Jean Miller's help in checking script and illustrations has been invaluable. My husband, Arthur Johnson, has produced all the diagrams and to him goes my gratitude for all his patience and encouragement.

For the patterns and items of lace listed below I am grateful to the following: 132, patterns by kind permission of Luton Museum and Art Gallery; 157, adaptation made and lace worked by the late Freda Bullock; 168, motif B lace made by Pamela Tyrrell; 172, lace made by Beryl Maw (pricking from Miss S.E. Dawson); 189, lace made by Ann Cope (pricking from the collection of the late Freda Bullock); 197, lace made by Joyce Symes; 236 & 239, lace made by Audrey Norman.

# 1 Introduction to Bucks Point Lace

## TRADITIONAL PATTERNS

The working of Bucks Point lace, particularly the elaborate designs, requires an understanding of the way in which prickings are made. There is a wealth of old traditional patterns available, some narrow and regular, others with flowing designs of scrolls, flowers and leaves. Many are beautiful and yet there are some, less attractive, which were probably altered by lacemakers in the second half of the nineteenth century in an attempt to make a pattern which could be worked more easily. In the past most of the lacemakers were the wives and daughters of agricultural workers and lace was made and sold to supplement the men's meagre earnings. Today, when the student of bobbin lace has mastered the techniques, he or she can choose a design and enjoy the challenge of working a wide variety of patterns. Those who made lace as a livelihood knew and worked only one or two patterns; they were limited by the need to produce a large quantity quickly and accurately.

Although much lace was made during the late sixteenth and seventeenth centuries little is known of the early designers. When the refugees came from Europe they brought their lace equipment and their patterns with them. As the cottage industry developed and increasing numbers of people were making lace, many new designs appeared. Usually, the patterns were given to the lacemaker by the dealer, who demanded that he should have the opportunity to purchase all the lace made from his pattern. Some of the dealers were designers and many of their patterns are in use today. John Millward, whose family had been lace dealers in the north of Buckinghamshire for several generations, was so aware of the poverty suffered in the villages around Olney that he designed 'rounds' or cap crowns in an attempt to create a new market. Between 1820 and 1829 he made many new designs and built up trade with America which lasted until the civil war in 1860. The rose, shamrock and thistle lace worn by Queen Victoria at her Accession in 1837 was designed by John Millward and made in Olney. The Lester family in Bedford were well known dealers and Thomas Lester (1835–1909) probably received more awards for lace designs than any other Englishman. His superb designs with flowers and leaves, and sometimes animals or birds, can be seen at the Cecil Higgins Art Gallery and Museum in Bedford. Many of the patterns have the plaited Beds-Maltese ground, but others have point ground, their intricacies daunting many experienced workers. As a dealer he employed women and girls who

showed exceptional skill; Lester's standards were high and inferior work was not accepted. It has been suggested that he worked many of his own designs but there appears to be little evidence to support this idea.

Many small associations were formed in an attempt to revive the craft at the end of the nineteenth century. The North Bucks Lace Association was one of the largest and most successful, its aims were set out as follows:

'To revive the ancient industry of Buckinghamshire Pillow Point Ground Lace which, owing to foreign competition, has practically disappeared throughout the County.

To assist the cottagers in their homes, by giving them regular employment, prompt payment, and freedom from the risk of uncertain sale.

To provide employment in the County and prevent migration to large centres.'

An attractive catalogue containing many photographed examples of lace was published; this is of particular interest to lacemakers today as many of the traditional names are stated. Pages from this catalogue are illustrated in photographs 1 and 195. In the price list which accompanies the photographs the following details are given:

| No. 1 | 'Carnation' | Mittens | £2 2s. od. per pair | (£2.10) |
|---|---|---|---|---|
| 2 | 'Oak Leaf' | Handkerchief | £1 9s. 9d. each | (£1.49) |
| 34 | 'Tulip' | Insertion | 15s. 9d. yard | (86p metre) |
| 35 | 'Tulip' | Edging | 16s. 9d. yard | (90p metre) |
| 42 | 'Tulip' | Edging | £2 10s. od. yard | (£2.61 metre) |
| 146 | 'Carnation' | Edging | 14s. od. yard | (76p metre) |
| 147 | 'Spray' | Edging | 10s. 6d. yard | (56p metre) |

A wide range of lace goods was offered for sale including berthas, cuffs, fans and scarfs, as well as edging and insertion. Gradually lacemaking became a leisure pursuit; no longer was it possible to sell fine bobbin lace at an economic price. Today many people enjoy the art and skills of lacemaking, working at the old patterns or creating new. The need for speed no longer exists; people aim for perfection and fine lace is made.

The designer kept patterns as 'drafts'; these are one or two pattern repeats pricked very accurately onto small pieces of tough vellum. The lacemaker usually made her own 14in (360mm) long pricking; originally it was the practice to prick onto vellum, but because it was very expensive prickings were later made on linen-backed card. Today a tough, heavy, glazed card is used. The Museum and Art Gallery at Wardown Park, Luton has a large collection of old drafts, many signed by the designers, as well as prickings, lace and equipment.

Very few new designs of Bucks Point lace are evident today, probably because there are so many attractive old patterns which are admired and worked with enthusiasm. Creating new designs takes a lot of time and lace is no longer a competitive trade. However, a study and analysis

of the principles of pattern making will give insight into the making of new designs as well as assisting in the working of old patterns. It is not practical to make the wide flounces of the eighteenth and nineteenth centuries, nor to produce a collar fashionable in a bygone age, but with knowledge of how the patterns were made it may be possible to adapt it for use today. Chapter 9 explains in detail the adaptation of old patterns and making of new.

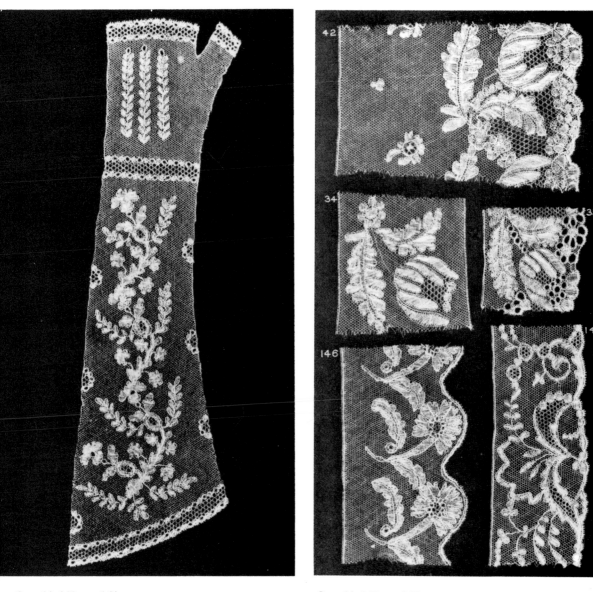

**One-third Natural Size**
1a MITTEN, 17in long. In Cream only

**One-third Natural Size**
1b EDGINGS

*The North Bucks Lace Association*

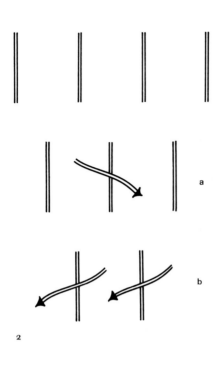

2

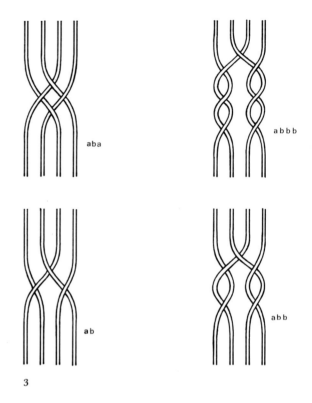

3

## BASIC INFORMATION

### Stitches

To clarify the terms used and the making of stitches refer to diagram 2. All stitches are made with two pairs of bobbins and depend on two movements:

*a* Pass the second thread over the third. This is known as *cross*.

*b* At the same time pick up the second and fourth threads and move them to the left over the first and third. This is known as *twist*.

(Refer to diagram 3.)

Cloth stitch *aba*  Ground stitch *abbb*
Half stitch *ab*  Honeycomb stitch *abb*

After making the ground stitch a pin is put in position. It is *never* covered. Honeycomb is worked by working a honeycomb stitch before and another honeycomb stitch after the pin.

### Working a simple pattern

Detailed instructions are given to revise and consolidate some of the basic techniques and to explain the working of the footside on both sides of the pattern. Should a length of insertion be required for a bookmark, instructions are given for beginning on page 98. The use of gimp thread is discussed in Chapter 3. Prepare the pricking, illustration 4, to work the insertion shown in photograph 5. Refer to diagram 6 and work as follows:

Hang a gimp pair on a pin at a. Hang five pairs on pins diagonally either side of pin a for the cloth diamond. It is unnecessary to twist these pairs as the twists are lost when

the support pins are removed. Pass the left hand side gimp thread between the threads of each pair, by passing it over the first thread and under the second. Pass the right hand gimp thread to the right by passing it under the first and over the second thread of each pair. The gimp is enclosed by giving each pair two twists, that is by passing the right thread over the left and repeating that movement.

### Cloth stitch

(Refer to illustration 3.) The bobbin movements are *aba*. Using the centre pairs work a cloth stitch and put up the pin between the pairs. In this situation, where there are the same number of holes on either side of the cloth shape, weaving may be started in either direction. However, it is sensible to develop the practice of always working in the same direction, unless the hole arrangement requires otherwise. This would occur if the hole on one side was higher (i.e. further back) than the other. Twist the pair that is to become the weaver twice. This is important as it enables the passive pair to be pulled straight and the weaver to lie closely round the pin. In this book the weaver will be worked to the right hand side, therefore when the centre pin is in position it is the left hand pair which is twisted and becomes the weaver. It will work in cloth stitch to the right through the centre pair and the next pair and the pin will be put in. The weaver remains the same pair throughout and it is always twisted twice as it passes round each pin. The cloth diamond is worked bringing in an extra pair before each pin as far as the widest part. Pairs are discarded after each pin as the diamond comes down to the point.

## Cloth stitch with hole

Refer to the second repeat on the pattern. When there is a six pin hole in a regular diamond shape it is necessary to work the first half of the diamond until there are two holes remaining on either side, (i.e. the point and the hole preceding it). In this pattern three holes will have been worked on either side. The weaver is brought back through the passive pairs to the centre; it is worked through the centre pair. In this pattern it is worked back through three pairs. Put in the pin between the centre pair and the weaver and cover the pin with cloth stitch. Both pairs are used to weave as shown in the diagram; they are twisted at the edge of the diamond and also at the pins which form the hole. When the pairs come together a cloth stitch is worked, the pin is put in and covered with a cloth stitch and one pair continues to weave and the other becomes a

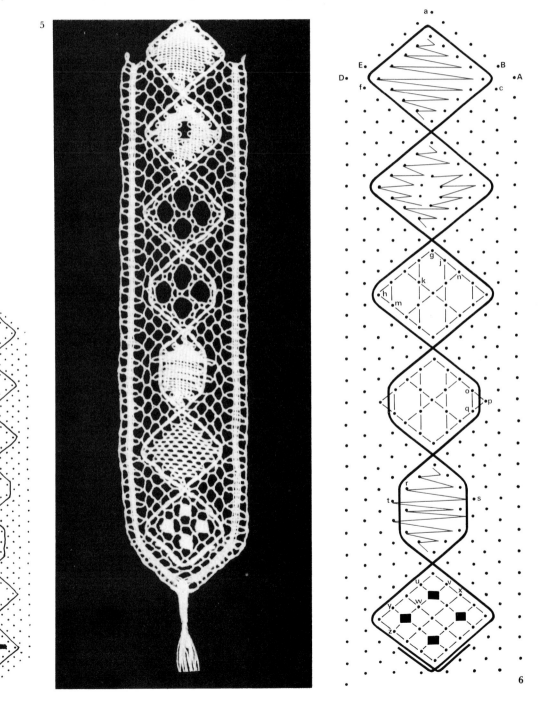

passive pair in the centre below the hole. When a six pin hole appears in a less regular shape, select three holes which are horizontally in line and work as described above. If the hole has more than six pin holes it will be necessary to use more holes on the outer edge of the cloth shape.

When the cloth diamond is complete the pairs are twisted twice and the gimp threads are passed through and crossed at the bottom. The pairs are twisted to enclose the gimp thread, the number of twists depending on the use of the pairs. As the pairs will be required for point ground they are twisted three times.

### Footside: to begin
Hang two pairs on pin A, one pair inside the other so that the adjacent threads belong to different pairs. Twist the threads on either side of the pin three times each; this forms a cord effect and is neater and stronger than separate threads. Work cloth stitch and three twists to cover the pin. (Refer to illustration 3.) Cloth stitch and three twists is worked *ababbb*. Note that three twists are given to both pairs. Ignore the outer pair (i.e. the right hand pair) and work in cloth stitch to the left through two pairs hung in order (side by side) on B. These pairs are the passive footside pairs and remain in this position throughout. Twist the weaver three times.

### Catch pin
The weaver and the next pair to the left (i.e. the pair from the point of the diamond) work a ground stitch. Put in the catch pin c to the right of both pairs.

### Point ground
When making Bucks Point it is usually referred to as 'ground'. Refer to illustration 3, and the stitch is worked *abbb*, cross and three twists. *Ground pins in Bucks Point lace are never covered.* Take the left hand pair from the catch pin and the next pair to the left and work a ground stitch; put the pin between the pairs. Discard the right hand pair and work the next ground stitch with the next pair to the left. Put up the pin and continue as far as the gimp line.

### Footside
Diagonal rows of ground are worked from the footside. Footside working always begins using the fourth pair from the outside edge.
  Take the fourth pair from the outside edge.
  Work two cloth stitches through the passive pairs towards the outside edge.
  Twist the weaver three times.
  Work cloth stitch and three twists with the outside pair; there must be three twists on *both* pairs of bobbins.
  Pin inside two pairs; there should be four threads lying to the outside edge of the pin.
  Ignore the outer pair.
  Work back through the two passive pairs in cloth stitch.
  Twist the weaver three times.
It is possible to put the pins into the pricking before working the catch pin stitch and the footside stitch; the finished result is the same and this is discussed in Chapter 5.

In England it is usual to work an edging with the footside on the right. An insertion requires the footside on both sides and on the left it is worked as follows. Refer to diagram 6 and hang two pairs on pin D. As at A, twist the threads three times and cover the pin with cloth stitch and three twists. Ignore the outer (left hand side) pair and work to the right through two pairs hung on E in cloth stitch. These are the passive pairs. Twist the weaver three times. Take the weaver and the next pair to the right and work a ground stitch, put up the catch pin to the left of both pairs. Take the right hand pair from the catch pin and the next pair to the right and work a ground stitch. The pin is put in between the pairs. Continue.

In this pattern work five diagonal rows of ground; the last row will consist of footside and catch pin only. Five pairs hang ready for the next diamond, the gimp threads are passed between the pairs and each pair is twisted twice, the number of twists being the same as in honeycomb stitch.

### Honeycomb
(Refer to illustration 3.) The bobbin movements are *abb*, pin, *abb*, using the same pairs. An area of honeycomb is worked in diagonal rows; it can be worked either from left to right or from right to left, but the hole farthest away must be worked first. In these instructions it is worked from right to left. Pairs enter diagonally from the ground to work the honeycomb stitch at the top, pin g is put in and covered with a honeycomb stitch. The right hand pair is discarded and another honeycomb stitch is worked with the next pair on the left. The pin is put in, and the stitch covered. Continue to pin h; this is known as the *continuous* row of honeycomb. Return to the right hand side and use a pair from the ground and the pair from pin g to work honeycomb stitch, pin j, honeycomb stitch. The next available pairs in the honeycomb work pin k and the other two pairs work pin m, as shown in the diagram. These stitches make the *gap* row. Return to pin n and work a continuous row; continue until the diamond is complete. Honeycomb is discussed in detail in Chapters 5 and 10.

In the next honeycomb shape the sides are straight, and the right hand pair from the gap row stitch o has to pass round the gimp and out to work ground pin p. Twists must be remembered before working the ground stitch. The pair passes back round the gimp thread, is twisted and is in position to begin the continuous row at q.

### Cloth stitch hexagonal shapes
When the gimp thread falls in a vertical line between cloth and ground, it is important to develop a method which will result in accurate ground and closely woven cloth. If the holes within the shape are used, the spaces between the weavers will be too great and the cloth will appear coarse and open. If the passive pair nearest to the gimp is taken out to work the ground stitch, and this is repeated several times, the cloth may appear sparse. Referring to diagram 6, weave from r through all the cloth pairs, and pass the gimp thread between the threads of the weaver, twist the weaver three times and work a ground stitch at pin s. The pin is put in to the left of both pairs as a catch pin, the left hand pair passes round the gimp and immediately weaves

back to t. There are no twists on the weaver between the cloth and the gimp as the intention is to achieve a solid effect. Pin t is worked as pin s. The catch pin always goes to the side of the pairs nearest to the gimp; in this way there can be a firm weaver and good tension is maintained.

## Half stitch

(Refer to illustration 3.) Half stitch is worked *ab*. A diamond in half stitch is worked in the same way as a diamond in cloth stitch. Although only one thread actually travels across the work, the pin is still put inside one pair (i.e. two threads).

## Tallies

In this pattern they are worked instead of certain ground pins and stitches. In order to understand and use the correct pairs for the tally, it is simpler to work as far as possible in diagonal rows. In this pattern begin at the top point of the diamond and work one row of ground diagonally to the left. Work pin v to begin the next diagonal row. Pairs from u and v make the tally. (Refer to illustration 7.) Take the second thread and weave it over the third and under the fourth. Bring it back over the fourth thread, under the middle one and over the left hand thread. To continue it passes across under the left and over the middle thread. It is important to keep the outside threads taut as they control the width of the tally. The weaving thread has to be supported throughout as it controls the shape. The weaving thread should be on the right hand side when the tally is complete. The left hand threads are twisted three times; similarly, the right hand threads are twisted and must be supported as any pull on the weaving thread will destroy the tally. The left hand pair from the tally works with the next pair for pin w. A tally is made with pairs from w and y and then pin z is worked. When the row from x is worked both tallies will be anchored firmly in position. To achieve good tallies the following points should be remembered:

7

1. The thread used for weaving must come from one side and finish on the other. If the ground row is worked from right to left, the weaving thread comes from the left and is twisted with the right hand thread as the tally is completed.

2. Always use the pair without the tally weaver for the stitch worked immediately the tally has been completed.

3. Always support the tally weaver until worked into the lace.

Should the lacemaker wish to use this insertion for some form of decoration, methods are suggested for beginning and ending in Chapter 9.

## Where to begin

This depends not only upon the lace design and the use for the finished lace, but also on the ability of the lacemaker and her understanding of the lace and pricking. Initially, it is most straightforward to begin by working the longest diagonal row of ground. This sets the pairs into the lace in an ordered way, and they will hang in the correct position ready to be used in the various pattern features. Refer to the simple edgings, for example Running River on page 15 and Pheasant's Eye on page 16. Extra pairs for the cloth trail in the Running River pattern are joined in at the discretion of the lacemaker, but in Pheasant's Eye a set number of extra pairs are required for honeycomb and joined in along the diagonal line. However, many patterns, including some simple edgings, cannot be started satisfactorily along one diagonal line. Refer to the Bean pattern on page 19; the ground can be worked ready to be taken into the honeycomb, but because of the honeycomb shape it is necessary to introduce pairs to begin the honeycomb shape and work in the ground pairs when they are required.

Occasionally a predominant feature, such as the diamond in the insertion pattern, is easy to work and the lacemaker may choose to set in the pairs where their use is obvious. Another advantage of choosing a feature that is outlined by gimp is the ease of joining when the lace has been completed. The threads will be fastened to the first stitches worked, and if these threads are laid along the gimp they may be sewn, almost invisibly, to the gimp and a strong join has then been made. When beginning more elaborate patterns, the flowers and other features are often worked and the ground introduced later where there are only a few ground stitches between the footside edge and pattern features. It is difficult to make a fine join that is strong across the net. (Refer to photograph 8.) The net (ground stitches) can be joined onto the pattern almost invisibly; there is only a narrow area at the footside and the join should not be too obvious. The pattern could have been started at the centre of one side, but this is inadvisable as one's eye travels to the centre as a focal point. (Pricking 9 accompanies the photograph.)

If the lace is required as length only, it may be quicker and neater to begin horizontally across the pricking; refer to the honeycomb fan pattern on page 20.

Specific shapes – the circles, squares, diamonds or hexagons – adopt different techniques in order to achieve the desired appearance. The edge may be a footside or with picots depending upon the use of the finished lace. (Refer to Chapter 9.) It is necessary always to begin the work with coupled bobbins, that is with a continuous thread without knots between the bobbins. Knots should be wound back onto one bobbin; they can be removed as the lace is made, and never appear in finished lace. (Refer to page 126.) The beginning of the work must be neat and accurate so that one can assess the suitability of the thread, appreciate the design more readily, and quickly achieve good tension as well as having the satisfaction of a tidy pillow.

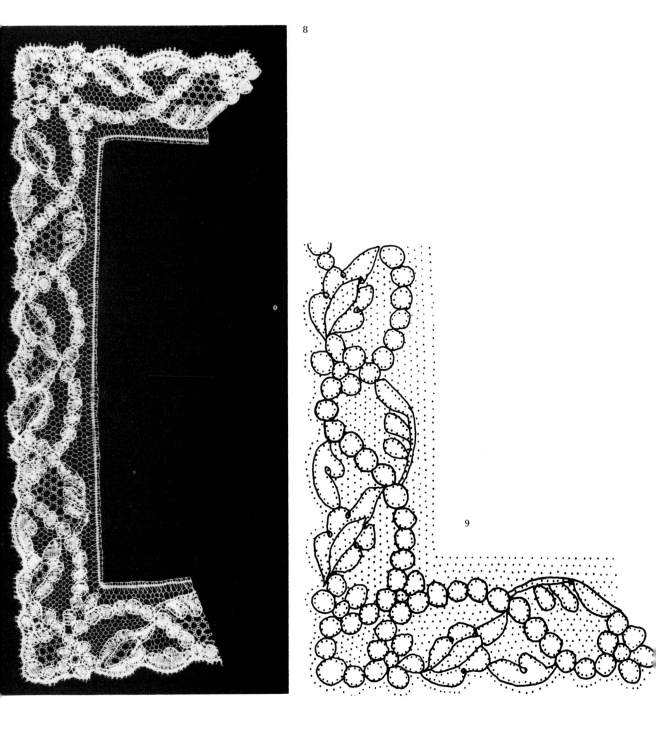

8

9

# 2 Nine Narrow Edgings

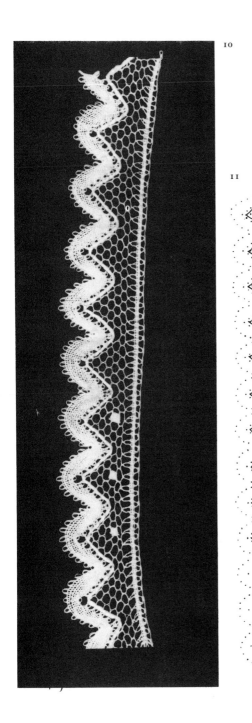

10

11

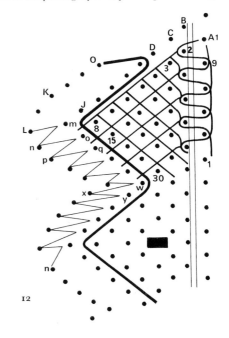

12

It is useful to have a collection of patterns for edgings that are easily made. Most narrow edgings are regular, requiring a set number of bobbins, and in each repeat of the pattern the number and arrangement of holes is the same. In the past many yards of lace would be made and then it was used as required. If used to trim cuffs, decorate boxes or edge handkerchiefs, it was gathered or mitred at the corners. Today the lacemaker demands the neat finish that is only achieved when a corner is worked in the lace and the footside changes direction. It will take longer to work the corner and move the lace on the pillow than to work extra length for gathering, but as lacemaking is no longer a means of livelihood the appearance is all important. Before working the corners in this chapter study Chapter 4.

## RUNNING RIVER
Running River is the name given to several similar patterns; they were most probably named by those old lacemakers who lived in cottages alongside the River Ouse which winds its way through the North Buckinghamshire villages. This version of Running River is an ideal pattern for a newcomer to Bucks Point lace; in the past it was made frequently by the younger children. It is worked in two parts, the ground and the trail, and is easy to understand. (Refer to the photograph 10, pricking 11 and diagram 12.)

## To work the footside and the ground

Hang two pairs on A1, two pairs in order on B and one pair on each pin from C to J inclusive. At pin A1 the two pairs would fall normally outside the pin, the pairs on B are the passives and the pairs on pins C to J would fall to the side of those pins as part of the ground. Attach a single gimp thread to a pin at O and bring it to the left of pin D, so that it passes between the remaining pairs to the left; these are the pairs that would come from the trail. Twist them three times each as they will be part of the ground. It is important to understand the reasons for hanging the threads in definite positions because, as soon as pin A is covered, all the stitches are worked in the usual manner for footside and ground. To cover pin A, twist the threads either side of the pin three times and work cloth stitch and three twists. Now imagine that the pin is to the left of these pairs. Ignore the outer pair; continue the footside sequence by working cloth stitch through the two passive pairs from B. Twist the weaver three times and work a ground stitch with a pair from C, put in the catch pin, 2, to the right of both pairs. Discard the right hand pair and work the next ground stitch with a pair hanging at D. Put up pin 3 between these pairs. Continue this diagonal row to the gimp line and pin 8. Remove the support pins from B to J. Work the ground as far as pin 30. Remember that the rows are always worked from the footside diagonally across the lace and that the footside is always worked beginning with the fourth pair from the outside edge.

## Gimp

Pass the gimp thread through the pairs on the diagonal line 8 to 30, moving it under and over the threads of each pair. Twist each pair twice so that they hang ready for the cloth stitch trail.

## The cloth trail

Hang five pairs in order on K and one pair on L. The pairs on K hang as pairs as they should enter the cloth smoothly and evenly. Use the pair on L as weaver and work in cloth stitch to the right through the five pairs from K. Twist the weaver twice and put up pin m to the left of the weaver. Use the same weaver throughout and weave back to the left through all the pairs. Put up a pin at n, twist the weaver twice and weave back through the five pairs already in the trail and through the pair from pin 8. Put up pin o to the left of the weaver and weave back to the outside edge and pin p. At q the weaver will have travelled through seven pairs, the six in the trail and one from pin 15; work on to pin w where the last ground pair from pin 30 is taken into the trail. The weaver travels to pin x. When it returns it will travel through one pair less to pin y; the pair that entered the trail from pin 30 will be left out after pin w. One pair is left out after each pin to achieve a balanced effect; these are required for the ground. Work to n. A common error made by the inexperienced lacemaker is to leave the weaver and weave back with the passive pair. This is avoided if one considers the situation and decides on pairs to be used when the weaver is at the outside edge.

## Avoiding possible faults

1. Ugly loops on the outside edge.
   a) increase the number of passive pairs in the trail.
   b) ascertain that two or three twists are put on the weaver at the edge.
   c) when working the second half of the trail encourage the bobbins to swing over to the left hand side of the pillow.
2. Thick, uneven trail.
   a) poor tension. It is essential to hold the weaver firmly and to pull the passive pairs down at the end of each row.

13

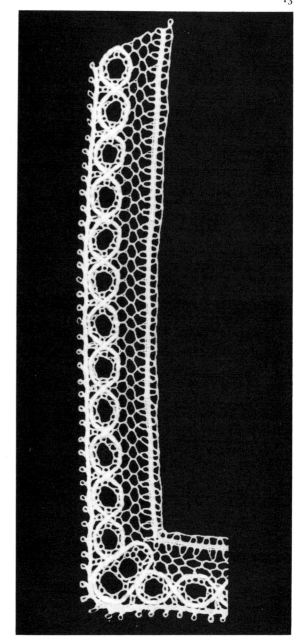

b)  too many passive pairs in the trail – unlikely to be the fault in this particular pattern.

c)  use of thread which is too thick for the pricking.

## Order of work

The trail is worked from n to n; the complete repeat of the trail is worked at one time. The ground is worked at one time; five diagonal rows are worked and it is started by taking the fourth pair from the edge out to work pin 1. Instructions for working the tally are given on page 13. To maintain a straight footside it is essential to leave the footside pins in the lace for the length of the pricking. However, the closeness of the pins and the weaving in the trail is inclined to extend the curve on the head, and the lace looks very attractive when mounted.

## PHEASANT'S EYE

This pattern is very quick to work and it can be adapted to make an attractive insertion. (Refer to photograph 13, pricking 14 and diagram 15.)

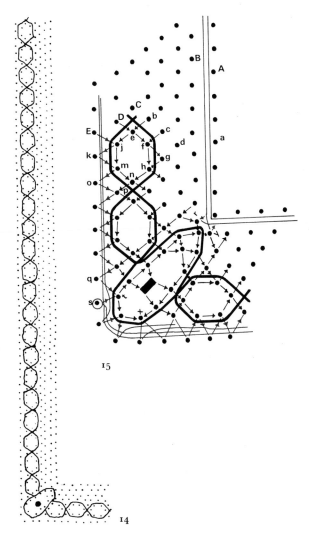

15

14

### Footside and ground

Work begins at pin A. Hang two pairs on A, two in order on B and one on each pin as far as C. If necessary refer to page 16 and work three rows of ground to pin d. Remove support pins. Note that pin g cannot be worked as the left hand pair for that pin must come diagonally from the left.

### The gimp

Hang one gimp pair on C and one pair on each of D and E. Pass the right gimp thread through pairs from b and c, and the left gimp thread through pairs from D and E. Twist the pairs twice as honeycomb stitches have two twists.

### Honeycomb ring

Take the centre pairs (i.e. the pairs from D and b) and work a honeycomb stitch, put up pin e and cover the pin. The two right hand pairs (i.e. the right hand pair from e and the pair from c) work honeycomb at pin f. Pass the gimp through the right hand pair from f, twist the pair three times and work a ground stitch with the pair from d at pin g. The left hand pair from g returns round the gimp, is twisted twice and works pin h with the pair from f. On the other side of the ring the two left hand pairs (i.e. the pairs from E and e) work a honeycomb pin at j. Remove support pins D and E. Replace the pin at E and hang on two more pairs in order; these will be used as the headside passive pairs. The gimp passes through the left hand pair from j and the pair is twisted twice. Use this pair to weave through the two passive pairs hanging on E in cloth stitch. Work the picot, k, as described below. Take this pair back through the two passive pairs in cloth stitch, twist twice, and pass the gimp through again. Twist twice more and work the honeycomb at pin m. Pairs from m and h work the honeycomb at pin n. Enclose the ring with gimp thread, crossing the gimp threads below pin n. Pairs from h and n require three twists, and pairs from m and n require two twists. The pair from m works in cloth stitch through the passive pairs, works a picot at o, travels back through the passive pairs to work honeycomb at pin p with the pair from n. The left hand pair from p works a picot and travels back for the next honeycomb ring.

One repeat is complete. Take the fourth pair from the footside edge and work out to begin the next diagonal row with footside pin a. Note that the passive pairs remain on the headside; it is important to achieve straight pairs and good tension.

### Corner

All corners in the chapter are as straightforward as possible and may be worked following the diagrams. However, this does not assist anyone to understand the method and it is recommended that Chapter 4 on corners be studied in order to gain insight into the reasons for the methods adopted.

Work as far as possible, completing the ring and including picot at q. Work the footside for the corner pin and the catch pin r. Make a false picot at s. Turn the pillow to the diagonal across the corner. Pass the gimp between the pairs as shown and twist the pairs afterwards for the honeycomb. Begin the honeycomb at pin t and complete

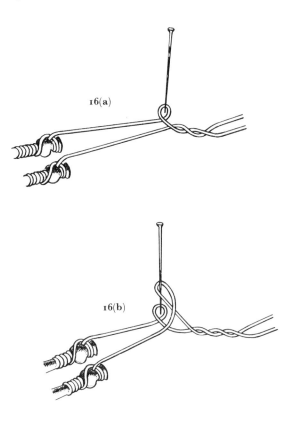

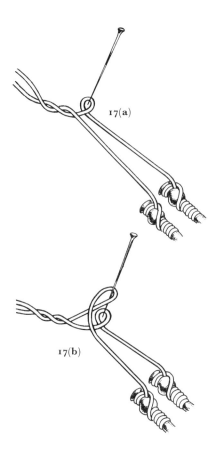

the oval at pin x. Note that the pair hanging from r becomes the outer passive and the present outer passive works the catch pin at y with the pair from u. The corner pin is used a second time. The changing of catch pin pair and outer passive is a common practice as it improves the appearance of the footside at the corner. The extra pairs joined in at a false picot will become additional passives on the headside and may be discarded.

## PICOTS

Only the double picot is acceptable in Bucks Point lace; it is worked as follows:

### 1. On the left side

(Refer to illustrations 16a and b.) Twist the pair three times. Take a pin in the right hand with the point towards the lacemaker; pass the pin under and over the outside thread and, leaving the thread very loose about the pin, put the pin into the picot hole. Now pass the inner thread loosely round the same pin in a clockwise direction. Twist the pair three times and pull gently but firmly so that the threads 'cord' together around the pin.

### 2. On the right side

(Refer to illustrations 17a and b.) Twist the pair three times. With the point of the pin towards the lacemaker, take the pin under and over the outside thread loosely.

Take the inner thread round the pin in an anticlockwise direction loosely. Twist the pair three times, and pull gently but firmly to 'cord' the twisted threads around the pin.

There is considerable variation in the number of twists used for picots. It is essential that the picot remains corded and does not split when the pin is removed. This depends not only upon the expertise of the worker but also on the thickness of thread, the size of the pin and therefore on the number of twists. When using fine thread, a tighter picot may be obtained using five twists before and two or three after the pin.

### 3. False picot

The false picot is used to imitate the picot when adding pairs at the beginning of a piece of work. It is also used to add extra pairs when working a corner, or an irregular lace. The pin is put into the picot hole and two pairs placed around the pin; they should fall one inside the other so that when each pair is given three twists a 'cord' effect is obtained. The pin is covered with cloth stitch and twists given as appropriate.

## BEAN

An old asymmetric pattern that is very satisfactory as a yard lace. When the corner was designed it became necessary to make the 'Bean' lie in reverse direction to

achieve a symmetrical corner. Pattern reversals are discussed in Chapter 4. (Refer to photograph 18, pricking 19
and diagram 20.)

It is usual to set in an edging along a diagonal line so that
the pairs in the ground lie ready to work the honeycomb or
cloth feature. However, this is not always possible and in
this case, although two rows of ground supply pairs for c
and d, there are no pairs available for a and b, as these
pairs come from a honeycomb area.

## Footside and ground

The row should be worked from A to provide the pair for c,
a second row is worked to provide the pair for d, and the
third row cannot proceed beyond pin e.

## Honeycomb Bean

Hang pairs outside the gimp to be brought in for pins a, b
and f. Pass a gimp through pairs required for f, a, b, c, d,
and work the Bean. The headside is worked in the same
way as the previous pattern. The diagram indicates the
position of the pairs in the honeycomb for the centre
feature and for the Bean shapes on either side.

## Corner

The extent of ground between the footside and the pattern
feature is greater in the Bean pattern than in Pheasant's
Eye and consequently the corner is more difficult to
arrange and to work. The arrangement is unusual in that
the gimp is taken out to the footside, but it is one way of
creating a neat corner that is simple to work.

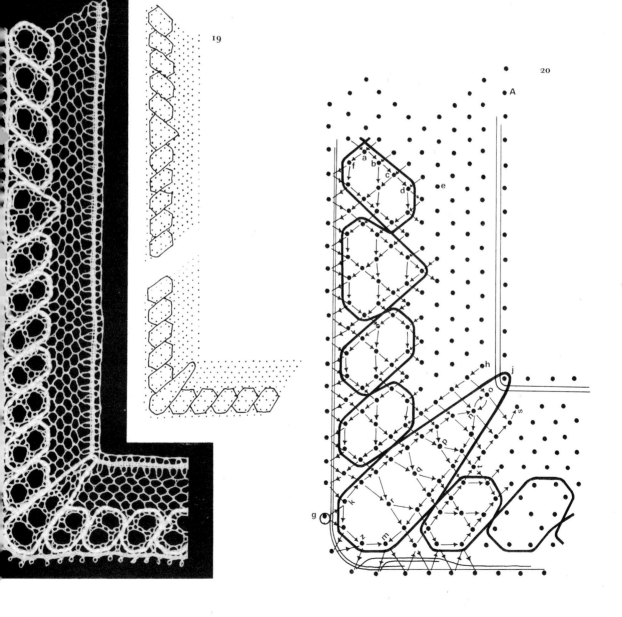

When the Bean has been completed, work the picot
honeycomb and second picot in preparation for the corner.
Make a false picot at g. Work from the catch pin h out to
the footside at the corner pin j, and leave both pairs at j on
the outside edge. Turn the pillow diagonally and take the
gimps through all the pairs as shown in the diagram. Begin
the honeycomb corner by working pin k. Work to the left
as far as z. Work to the right to pin o. Remove pin n and
work a honeycomb stitch with the pair at that pin and the
pair returning from o, replace the pin and cover it. Work
the gap row stitches and complete the honeycomb at m.
The right hand gimp thread weaves through the two
passive pairs, round the corner pin and back through the
passive pairs, and on through the pairs to enclose the oval
honeycomb shape. The extra pairs added as a false picot
are discarded in the headside passives. The inner pair at
pin j works through the two footside passives in cloth stitch
in preparation for the catch pin at s. This cannot be
worked until the next Bean has been started. The pair from
the honeycomb works ground stitch t, and the Bean is
completed. Work from t to s and then complete the ground
rows as required.

## HONEYCOMB FAN
This is a popular pattern as it can be worked with several
variations. (Refer to photograph 21, pricking 22 and
diagram 23.) It has been started along a horizontal line in
order to explain this method of beginning a pattern. In
addition detailed instructions are given for working picots
on a curved head.

### To begin along a straight edge
Hang three pairs on A and two pairs on each of pins B to H
inclusive. Twist the threads that hang either side of the pin
three times each to create the twisted 'cord' behind the pin.
   *To work ground.* Use the left hand pair from G and the
right hand pair from H to make a ground stitch and put up
pin b between the pairs. Take the left hand pair from F
and the pair from G to work the ground stitch and pin c.
Complete the diagonal row by working the ground stitch
and pin d. Work diagonal rows from the top, from pins F
and E to e, E and D to f, D and C to g, and C and B to h.
Although the honeycomb fan can be worked now, instructions are given for the footside as this is part of setting in the
ground and footside.
   *To set in the footside.* Twist the two right hand threads on
A three times and work cloth stitch and three twists with
the next pair to the left, also hanging on pin A. Ignore the
right hand pair and take the left in cloth stitch through the
third pair on A and through the remaining pair on B; these
two pairs become the footside passives. Twist the weaver
three times and work a ground stitch with the pair hanging
ready and put up the catch pin at i. Continue the ground
row as required.

### Gimp
Hang a gimp pair on a support pin and take it through the
seven pairs entering from ground.

## Use of false picots when setting in the head
Assess the number of pairs required to work the headside.
With reference to the diagram it can be seen that five pairs
are needed for the honeycomb and two more for the passive
pairs. It is convenient to set in pairs from false picots, but
one is restricted to an even number of pairs. In this pattern
the first pair to enter the honeycomb on the left is brought
in over a gimp thread. False picots are made at k, l and m
and used as indicated in the diagram. The right hand pair
of the false picot at k enters the honeycomb. The right hand
pair from the false picot at l enters the honeycomb and the
left hand pair works one cloth stitch with the pair from k.
At m the right hand pair works into the honeycomb and

21

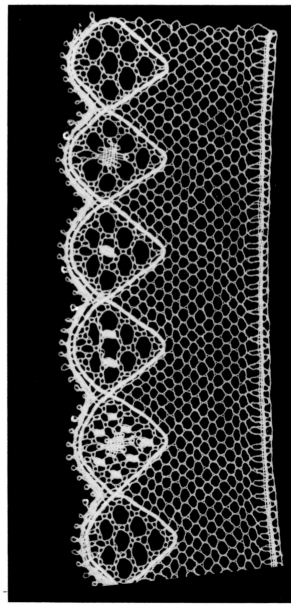

the left hand pair works a cloth stitch with the pair next to it. The third pair from the picot edge works out through the two cloth pairs to make picot n. The honeycomb is worked according to the diagram, all rows being worked from right to left, alternating *continuous* and *gap* rows. If necessary, refer to page 76. Complete the fan but not the picot edge; the last picot worked will be at pin p.

## Headside method of working

The method applies to most Bucks Point patterns; it is possible in very many patterns to work the complete curve at one time. This avoids a lot of bobbin movement across the pillow, and clarifies the order of work.

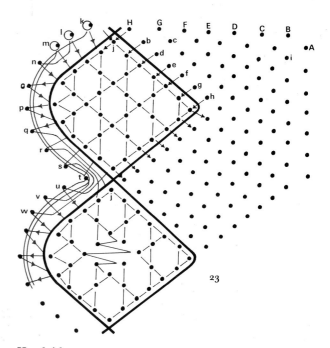

23

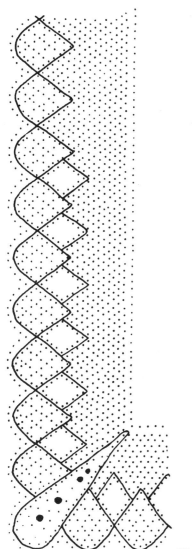

22

## Headside sequence

Take the first pair hanging from the honeycomb and work out through the passive pairs to work picot q. Work back through two cloth pairs and leave it in position untwisted. Take the next pair and work out to picot r, make the picot and work back through two cloth pairs only. Work out to picots s and t similarly, each time returning through two cloth passive pairs only. The last pair hanging from the bottom point of the honeycomb is worked out through all the pairs to the edge and makes the picot at u, and is brought back through two pairs only. At this time count the number of picots that require working to provide pairs for the honeycomb. With reference to the beginning it will be seen that four picots were used, k, l, m and n. In the curve being worked now, t and u have been completed and therefore two more picots are required. Take the pair which worked picot u (it is lying third pair from the edge) and work two more cloth stitches. The gimp travels to the left through two passives and this pair. The two pairs between the gimp and passive pairs are used to make the two picots at v and w. Take the third pair from the edge, work out to the edge, make picot v and come back through the cloth pairs and the gimp for the honeycomb. Similarly, take the third pair once more, work out to make picot w and back through the cloth pairs and gimp to the honeycomb.

It is important to understand this sequence as it is crucial to the success of the headside. The principle is to take, in order, each pair to the edge, work a picot and return through *two* pairs only. When all pairs have been used, take the last picot pair through the two passives and on through the same number of passive pairs as there are picots still to be made. Complete picots by taking the *third* pair out to make the picot and then bringing it back all the way to the gimp.

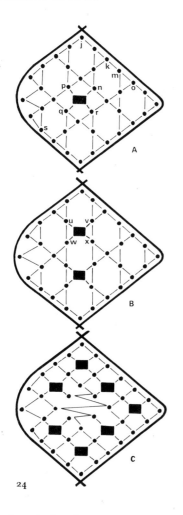

24

continuous row from o to anchor the other side of the tally at r as soon as possible; s must be worked before that row can be completed.

3. Tally in place of holes in the honeycomb (refer to diagram 24(b)). This is easy to understand as the pairs that work a particular pin are used to make the tally. The top continuous and gap row including pin u is worked. Work the next continuous row to include pin v. The tally is worked with pairs from the gap row stitch u and the continuous row previous stitch v. Again use a thread from the left for the weaver and leave it on the right. Complete the continuous row, working pin w, etc. Work the gap row where pin x will anchor the tally firmly.

25

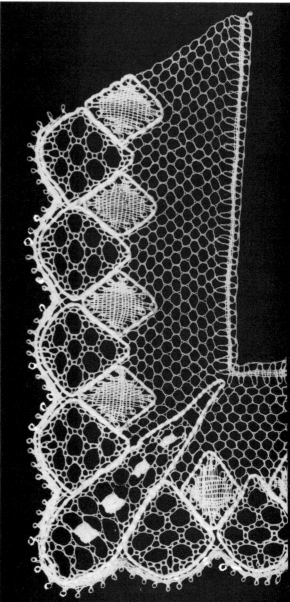

## Corner

This pattern is worked on the same arrangement of holes as Duke's Garter; the corner on page 23 is suitable for both patterns.

## Variations in honeycomb

Refer to diagrams 23 and 24 and mark the pricking as necessary.

1. Mayflower (refer to diagram 23). It is necessary to understand honeycomb and the position of the threads. Work the continuous rows in both directions from j. Work two gap row stitches in each direction. The six pairs are available for the cloth diamond. When complete remember to twist the pairs twice before the honeycomb is completed.

2. Tally in the centre of a honeycomb ring (refer to diagram 24(a)). Work the honeycomb in diagonal rows as far as and including the row beginning at pin k. Work pins m and n in the gap row and use the pairs from p and n to make the tally. The tally weaver should come from the left hand pair as it will be left on the right to be used later. Pin q is worked immediately after the tally is complete to keep it in position and in good shape. It is good practice to leave the other stitches in the gap row until later and begin the

4. Mayflower and tallies (refer to diagram 24(c)). Many effects are possible; in this fan the tallies are worked within the honeycomb rings about a mayflower.

## DUKE'S GARTER (1)

An old traditional pattern to which a corner has been added for those lacemakers who wish to make handkerchief edgings. (Refer to photograph 25, pricking 22 and diagram 26.) The pattern is worked in the same way as the honeycomb fan pattern; the only difference is the cloth diamond and the gimp thread which encloses it. Note that the gimp which travels round the curve of the honeycomb fan encloses the diamond completely and returns to travel round the head of the next fan.

### Corner

Refer closely to diagram 26. Three pairs extra are required; the picots are worked in the usual way with available pairs. A false picot is made at a; this also provides for a picot at b. To provide the pair for picot c, a single pair was hung over the gimp and worked out to the edge through the two passive pairs. This is not good practice as it may distort the gimp line; however, it is quick and easy. The alternative is to join in two pairs as a false picot and keep the second as an extra passive. The honeycomb is started at d and worked to the right as far as e. The middle holes are worked as in the diagram and the continuous row worked back to finish at f; g and h are worked as gap row stitches. As the picot edge is worked the number of passive pairs increases and the extra pairs are discarded.

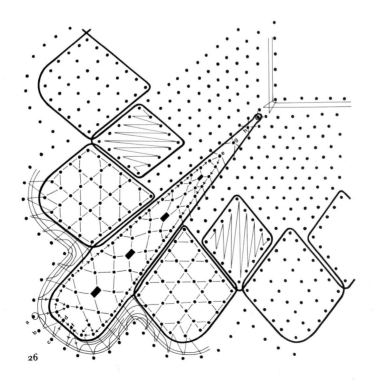

26

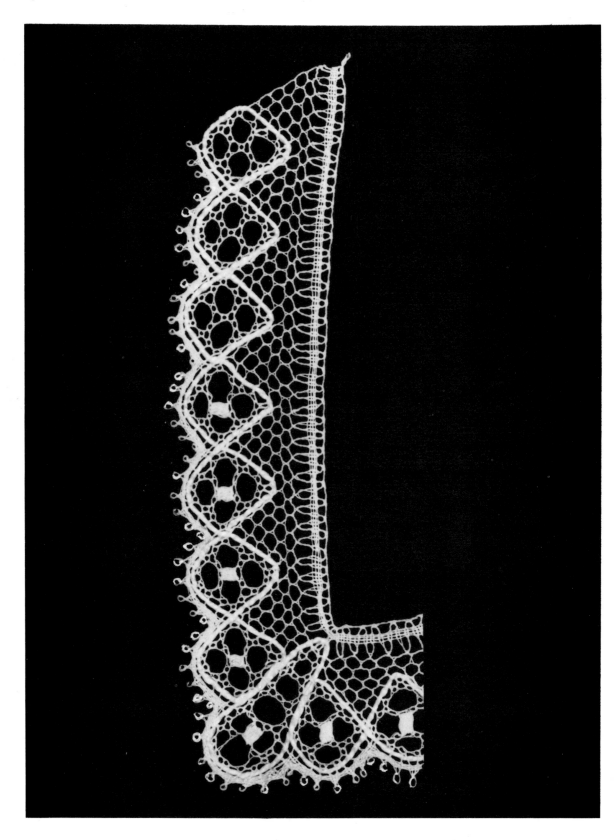

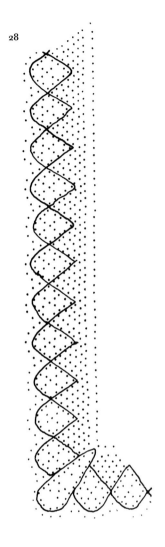

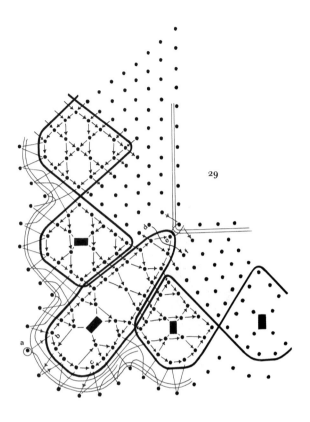

## SMALL HONEYCOMB FAN

A small honeycomb fan can be worked very speedily and for variety a tally can be set in the centre. Traditionally it has been worked alternately with four honeycomb buds as an attractive edging. (Refer to photograph 27, pricking 28 and diagram 29.) The diagram explains the method of working the straight edging.

### Corner

An extra pair is required to work pin b. One pair could be hung over the gimp as described in a previous pattern, but the better way is to make a false picot at a and carry the extra pair as a headside passive. Honeycomb is worked from b and completed at c. The tally is necessary to fill a space as the honeycomb stitches are rather far apart. The pair from d is superfluous to requirement and must be taken neatly across the corner. It passes round the gimp and works cloth stitch and two twists with the pair travelling to e. After pin e has been worked it makes cloth stitch and two twists with the pair in the honeycomb as it leaves e, passes round the gimp and is ready for pin f which cannot be worked until the corner is complete. The honeycomb is completed at c. The extra pairs are discarded from the headside passives.

30

31

## HONEYCOMB FAN AND RINGS

(Refer to photograph 30, pricking 31 and diagram 32(a).)
At first sight the pattern appears irregular, but upon closer
scrutiny it is seen that the rings have been reduced by
omitting the top pin in the first ring and the bottom pin in
the lower ring. This reduces the length of the ring feature
until it matches the length of the fan, making the pattern
more attractive. The rings on either side fit into the space of
a four pin bud, but by careful placing of two holes on the
inner point instead of one, the illusion of a rounded bud or
ring has been created. There is much to be learnt from
studying old prickings and attempting to find the reasons
for the old designers use and arrangement of holes. In this
case each ring has been reduced by the width of one row of
ground, i.e. three rows altogether, which leaves five rows to
provide the required pairs. The fan requires pairs from five
rows of ground, therefore both features are the same
length.

### Edging

The diagram gives the working method. Note that the
honeycomb in the top ring is not joined across the top, but
worked independently from the two top pins. On the inner
edge of the side rings, work pin chain; that is, they make the
honeycomb stitch and the pin is put in and covered, and
immediately a second pin is put in below and covered.
(There are three stitches and two pins, the stitches made
with the same pairs.) Also note that the left hand side gimp
from the top ring works round both side rings to avoid an
unsightly hole in the centre.

### Corner

An extra gimp pair is added for the four stitches which
separate the ground on either side of the corner. Work the
last row of ground from catch pin a to b. Work ring A,
working the holes in the order shown on the diagram.
Work the first three honeycomb pins from the corner; these
have an independent gimp thread. Work ring B in the
order shown, releasing a pair to complete the row of four
honeycomb stitches, and bringing it back to complete the
ring. A false picot is introduced at E and ring C is

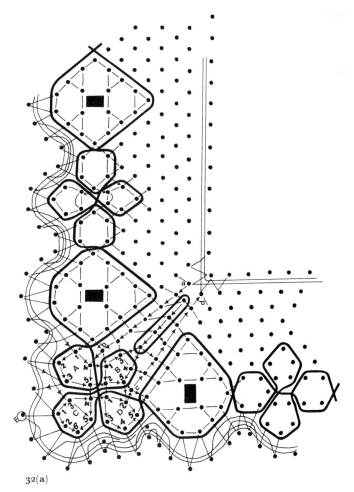

32(a)

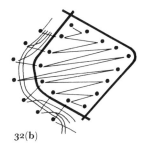

32(b)

33

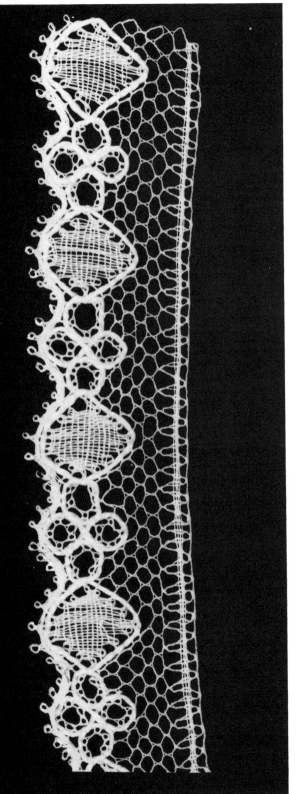

34

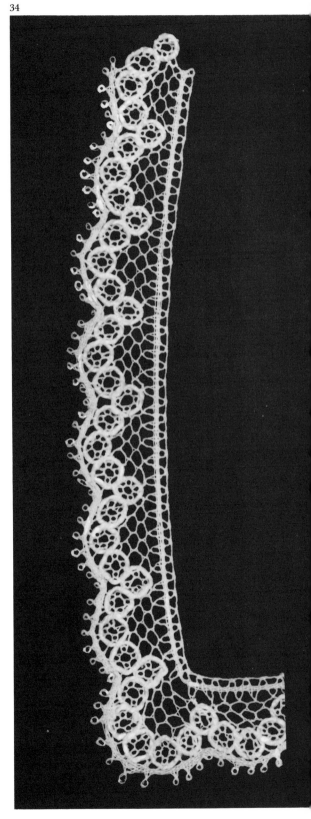

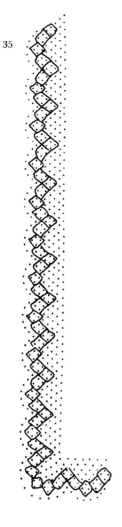

35

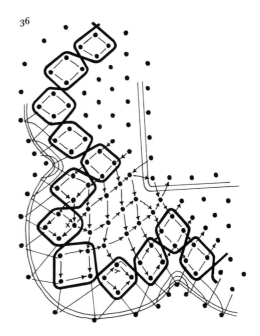

36

completed. Work ring D. From the ground stitch at pin c, work down to the catch pin d. Note that the pair from catch pin a became a passive pair and the passive from the previous edge becomes the right hand pair for the catch pin d.

## DUKE'S GARTER (2)

This pattern has the same arrangement of holes as the previous one, but the fan is worked in cloth stitch. (Refer to photograph 33.) Pricking 31 is used but the holes within the fan edge are omitted. Diagram 32(a) is relevant and the same corner is used for both patterns. In practice the corner given for the small honeycomb fan pattern can be worked, but the design is not in keeping with the four rings of the latter patterns. Diagram 32(b) gives the method of working the cloth fan. In order to keep a close and even cloth effect the weaver is taken out through the gimp to work the picot and brought back to continue weaving. There are no twists between the cloth fan and the weaver but there are two twists between the weaver and the passive pairs. This method is considered by some people to be technically incorrect, as the usual method is to take the cloth pair in the fan, that is adjacent to the gimp, out to work the picot and

back to be taken into the cloth fan again. This leaves a hole which, in a narrow regular pattern, is very obvious. The choice depends on the pattern and must be made at the discretion of the lacemaker.

## BEAD PATTERN

A well chosen gimp thread enhances this pattern. It is very simple and depends on a fairly thick gimp thread. Refer to photograph 34, pricking 35 and diagram 36. To increase the width and add interest a cucumber foot may be added; this is described on page 73.

### Corner

This requires the addition of one pair at x. Work the honeycomb stitch and put up pin x. Now hang a pair over the gimp thread and the two threads to the right of the honeycomb pin and allow it to fall outside the gimp ready for the ground stitches. Cover the honeycomb pin x, keep the threads taut and complete the four pin bud. The spare pair appears at y. Carry it alongside the gimp for about 25mm (1in) and then discard it. This method of disposing of threads is discussed in Chapter 10.

# 3 The use of gimp threads

Gimp thread must be soft and shiny to outline the pattern and enhance the design. Linen floss is excellent but, today, is difficult to obtain. Pearl cotton is a satisfactory substitute; it is made in two sizes suitable for Bucks Point lace, number 8 and number 12. The gimp thread gives definition to a pattern feature or it may be used to create a particular effect within the ground. By tradition the gimp is the same colour as the rest of the lace; white lace always has a white gimp and ecru lace has an ecru gimp. Number 12 pearl cotton is recommended for use with most of the fine threads we have today. A highly twisted thread, such as crochet cotton, is unsuitable as it is harsh and does not lie very flat.

## USE OF GIMP

1. Gimp threads are passed through a pair as follows:
   from left to right it moves under the first thread and over the second;
   from right to left it moves over the first thread and under the second.
2. With very few exceptions gimps are enclosed by twists on pairs either side. It is usual to twist pairs to enclose gimp threads as follows:
   when the pair is to be used in ground it receives three twists;
   when a pair is to be used for honeycomb stitch it receives two twists;
   when a pair is to work cloth or half stitch it receives two twists.
3. Gimp threads may be crossed right over left or left over right according to the preference of the lacemaker. It is important for the appearance of the finished work to be consistent and always cross in the same direction.
4. When two gimp threads lie together they may be treated as one or separated by twists. They are kept together as a single gimp in most geometric patterns; for example, refer to Duke's Garter on page 23, or the trefoil pattern on page 24. In floral patterns when it is important for effect to separate the petals of flowers, or create a break between pattern features, the twisting of pairs between gimps is at the discretion of the lacemaker.
5. Some lacemakers have difficulty in understanding the moving of gimp threads. If this is so, forget the gimp threads and concentrate on the moving of the pairs of threads which create the pattern. The pairs

**37**

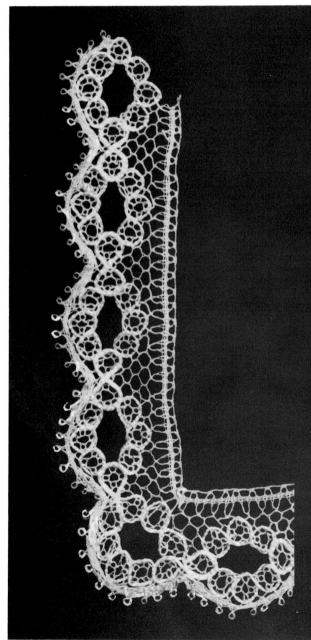

usually move diagonally from one stitch or shape to the next. If there is a black gimp line on the pricking and a gimp thread between the two features, take the pair round the gimp thread and continue. Twists are given to the pair before and after it has negotiated the gimp thread.

Difficulties should not arise regarding the position of the gimp thread as it has, as a guide, the black line on the pricking. The many pairs of threads in the lace will move as required, and when necessary will pass round the gimp and continue to make the pattern. Lace takes many hours to make and therefore it is essential to mark the pricking very carefully and to understand the path of the gimp threads before beginning to work. A dozen patterns are included in this chapter, each one emphasising a different situation which requires a specific treatment.

## RING OF RINGS

This shows the use of two pairs of gimps which enclose four pin honeycomb buds arranged to form a circle. The dominant feature of the pattern is the hole in the centre of the rings. (Refer to photograph 37, pricking 38 and diagram 39.)

### To work bud a

Follow the diagram and work the bud using one gimp pair. Do not cross the gimps at the bottom; leave them side by side. Introduce a new gimp pair and pass it through all four pairs from bud a as shown. Cross the gimps ready for buds b and e.

### To work bud b

Using pairs from bud a and pairs from the ground work bud b and cross the gimps below the centre pairs.

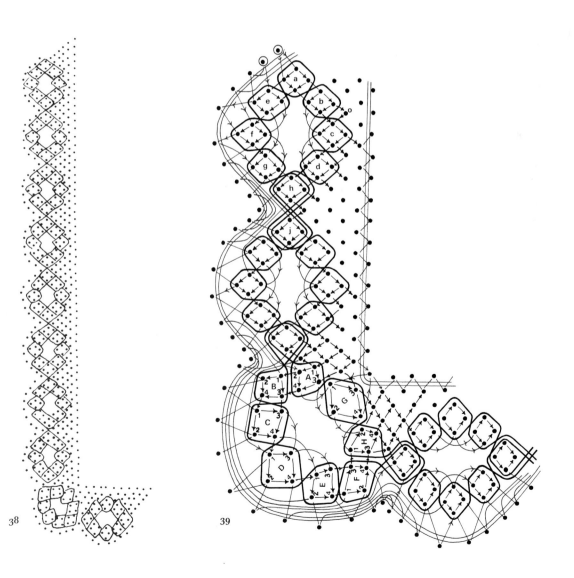

38          39

## To work bud c

Two ground rows are worked in preparation for this bud. Note that the ground pin o is worked with a pair from bud b. The right hand pair from the bottom of b provides the top pair for bud c. The other pair from the bottom of b is put alongside the gimp thread and carried almost invisibly until required. The pair from the left side of b is brought round and into the side in c.

## To work bud d

One more row of ground must be worked. On the other side of the bud, the pair from the bottom of c goes into the top of d. The other pair for the top of d comes from b and is the pair carried alongside the gimp. It is twisted twice and passes round the gimp and into the bud. The pair from the side of c works the side of d.

Work buds e, f, and g similarly to the buds on the right hand side.

## To work bud h

Cross the gimps that lie at the bottom of buds g and d. The right hand gimp thread from bud g travels on to the right through four pairs, i.e. two from g and two from d. Similarly the left hand gimp from d travels to the left through four pairs, i.e. two from d and two from g. The other gimp threads fall naturally on either side of h. Only two threads cross above the bud. Work bud h and cross both gimps, keeping them together for j.

## Corner

The diagram clarifies the method and order of work. Buds are worked in letter order from A to H and within each bud the order of working the pins is indicated numerically. The weaver from the corner foot pin is used for the first pin in G and from pin 4 in G returns to the footside and the same corner pin.

## RAM'S FACE

The pattern explains the use of gimp in ground for decorative purposes. Such arrangements are known as fingers of gimp, and the simplest form to work is shown here. (Refer to photograph 40, pricking 41 and diagram 42.) The pricking must be marked carefully to indicate the path of the gimp in the ground. The last pattern repeat has a cloth diamond with a hole in the centre; this is an alternative form of the pattern. Instructions for working a six pin hole in cloth are given on page 139; the weaver must pass out round the gimp to work one ground stitch on the right hand side.

## To work the ground and gimp fingers

In the working diagram the arrows are marked on the second repeat so that on the first pattern the uninterrupted gimp lines are seen clearly. Work the honeycomb as far as possible and the outside pair out to picot a, work the pair back through the passives and round the gimp for use later. Work a diagonal ground row to b. Work four more rows of ground, the first row to c, while the other rows are left diagonally from c.

Take the right hand gimp thread through six pairs to the right; this includes the pair from c. Twist the last two pairs three times, work a ground stitch and put up pin d. Take the gimp through the pairs required for e (it travels through three pairs to the left), twist the last pairs three times and work a ground stitch and put up pin e.

The gimp travels to the right through four pairs (two from e, one from d and one from the ground). Twist the last two pairs three times and work a ground stitch and put up pin f. The gimp travels back to the left through five pairs, and all five pairs receive three twists each. The last two pairs work a ground stitch and pin g is put in position. Ground stitches are worked and pins h and i are put in; there is no link between these pins.

**40**

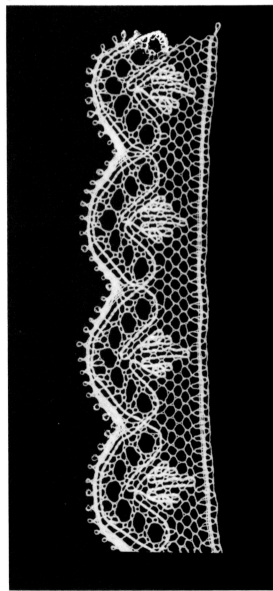

The gimp travels to the right through seven pairs (two from each of g, h and i and one from the ground). Before ground stitches n, m, k and j are made, the necessary twists must be put on all pairs. When the stitches are worked and the pins are in position the gimp thread travels to the left in preparation for the ground stitch and pin o. Pairs from m and n work the stitch for pin o. The twists are given and stitches and pins p and q are completed.

By following the diagram closely, pins r, s and t are completed. Without additional twists the gimp travels to the left to include pairs from b and n required for u. Twists are given to the pairs required for u and for the row of ground from u; this is completed to v. Pairs from j, r and t are twisted and two more ground rows worked to w and x.

The second half of the honeycomb can be worked completely. It is usual to allow the gimps to fall together; twists are not put between them. For example, there are no twists between r and t, other than the twists which are part of the ground stitch at r and those used to enclose the double gimp before the stitch for pin t is in position. The gimp thread must be kept taut and the stitches should be firm and tight to achieve a clear effect.

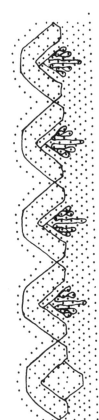

41

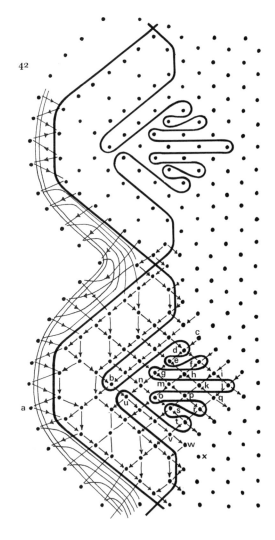

42

## TREFOIL

This pattern illustrates the use of gimp to achieve a close neat trefoil centre. (Refer to photograph 43, pricking 44 and diagram 45.) The same gimp thread is used to enclose features on both sides of centre, in this case the stem c and the bud d. The double gimp thread makes the stem remain as one thread; there are no twists between the gimps.

### Order of work

The pin at a is enclosed with honeycomb and the gimp threads are crossed below the pin. Honeycomb ring b is completed and the gimp threads are crossed and left between the bottom pairs. The diagonal row of ground to the right of b is worked and the gimp thread is brought to the right through six pairs; the ground stitch is worked and pin c is put in position. The gimp thread is brought back to the left to include the pairs required for bud d. There are no twists separating gimp threads between b and d. When bud d has been completed, the gimp encloses it and returns to centre, the gimps are crossed and bud e is worked. Pin f is enclosed with honeycomb and surrounded by gimp, then bud g is worked. Stem h is completed and the same gimp encloses bud j. Finally bud k is worked. The order of work is indicated on the diagram; the stems and buds are in alphabetical order. The arrangement of gimp threads is similar in Duke's Garter on page 27.

Any insertion may be increased in width by the addition of cucumber foot. Refer to Chapter 5.

43

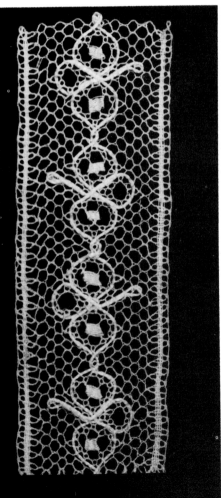

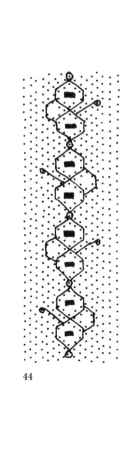

44

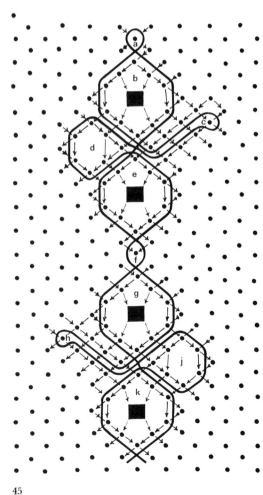

45

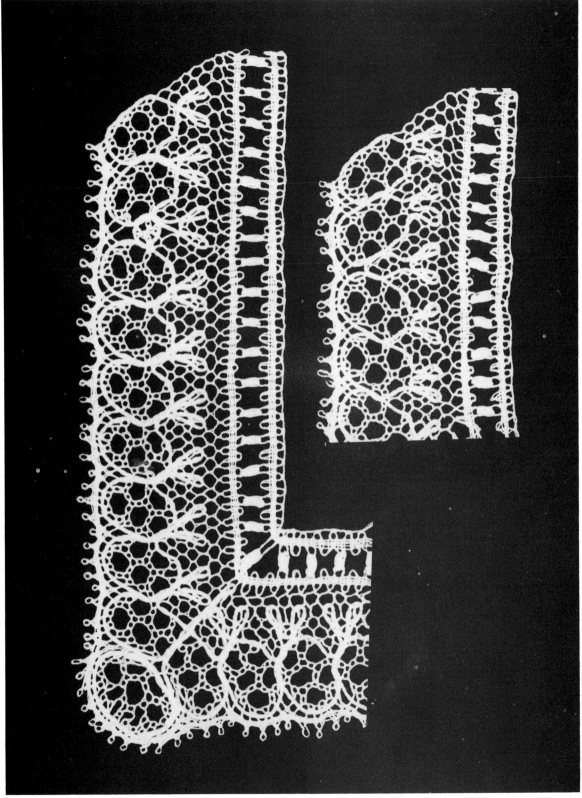

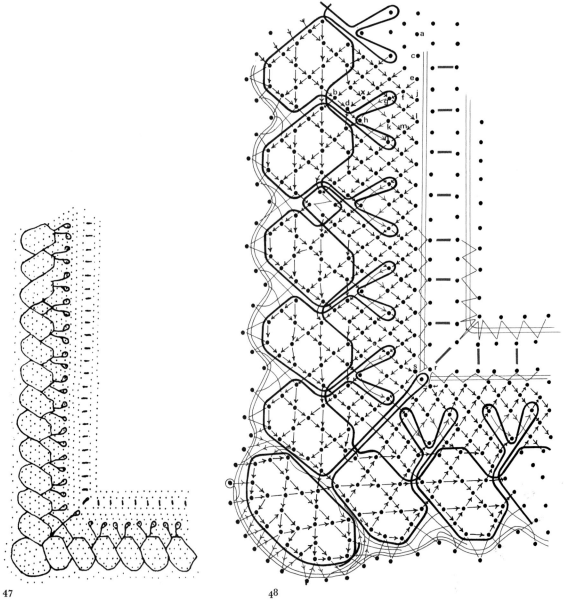

47

48

## PATTERN WITH HONEYCOMB, FINGERS IN GROUND AND CUCUMBER FOOT

Frequently the holes are missing along the gimp in the ground; this gives a softer effect and yet emphasises the fingers. (Refer to photograph 46, pricking 47 and diagram 48.) As an edging the pattern can be worked with the honeycomb lying in either direction. Here it is shown with a corner and a centre feature to reverse the design. To achieve a crisp and neat result the honeycomb must be enclosed completely; the fingers should be worked before or after the honeycomb but not allowed to break the continuous gimp line. The inset in photograph 46 shows the error.

### Cucumber foot

This is described on page 74.

### Fingers in ground

Refer to diagram 48 and work the rows of ground from a to b, c to d, and e to f. Take a gimp through the pairs from b to the right to include one pair from f and twist the last two pairs three times in order to work the ground stitch and put up pin g. Take the pair from x which has no twists and the pair from g which is twisted and work together in cloth stitch. Take the gimp back through the right hand pair from g, the two pairs which made a cloth stitch and the right hand pair from d. Twist all pairs three times. Work the ground stitch using the right hand pair from d and the left hand pair from the cloth stitch. Put up pin h.

Work the ground rows j to k and l to m. Take the same gimp (at present to the left of h) and put it through both pairs from h, the pair hanging from k and the left hand pair from m. The pairs from h and k remain untwisted and work together in cloth stitch. Twist the right hand pair and the pair from m and work ground stitch and put up pin n. Take the gimp back to the left through all the hanging pairs and through the five pairs on the left waiting to work the honeycomb. The other gimp thread moves to the right through pairs from b, d, and h. The working diagram clarifies the gimp position and that there are three gimp threads together below b, d, h. Note that there are twists on either side of gimp threads but not between them. The cloth stitch within the gimp should lie smoothly and therefore there are no twists before cloth stitches other than the twisted pair which has worked the ground stitch to hold the finger in position.

Below the centre feature the honeycomb is worked completely before the ground and fingers. Also note that the same gimp thread travels round the head side curve in every pattern.

### Honeycomb

The oval shape is not bounded entirely by continuous rows. This presents no problems; the honeycomb is completed and the pairs will fall into position, both in and out of the oval, without difficulty.

### Corner

This corner can be worked following the diagram. It is necessary to add two pairs as a false picot, also to carry one pair (shown in blue) with the gimp across the corner. The weaver on the inner trail of the cucumber foot works the tally from r before the catch pin at s. When the corner is complete and catch pin t is in position the weaver passes round pin r for the second time.

## HEART AND GARLAND

This emphasises the need to use a minimum number of gimp threads to completely enclose pattern features. It also clarifies the method for working honeycomb stitches between gimps on vertical and diagonal lines. (Refer to photograph 49, pricking 50 and diagram 51.)

### Gimp threads

One pair remains on the headside enclosing the row of honeycomb stitches, the heart and the triangle which separates the repeats. The other pair works the four pin buds.

*The headside gimp pair.* The outer (left hand side) gimp thread encloses the triangle and returns to the outside edge. It also encloses the heart and works a nook pin at u (nook pins are discussed later in this Chapter). Pin u is worked as follows: the weaver from t works back through three pairs in cloth stitch; the gimp thread passes through twisted pairs from h and j and then on through the next pair which has been twisted also; it continues through the untwisted weaver, the weaver and the pair to the right of it work a cloth stitch and pin u is put up and closed with a cloth stitch; the gimp thread passes back through the untwisted weaver and the weaver works to the left to pin v; the pair hanging at u is twisted twice, the gimp is passed through and it receives two more twists, ready to be taken into the cloth by the weaver from v. When a nook pin is worked the passive pairs are twisted throughout but the weaver is never twisted.

*The gimp which surrounds the four pin buds.* The threads must be pulled tightly to achieve definite buds. If preferred, the right hand gimp from the triangle and the left hand gimp from the bud may be crossed to link both sides of the pattern together.

### Honeycomb

The arrangement of honeycomb holes within the gimp threads are continuous with those in the rest of the pattern, the only discrepancy being the extra holes at x and y. The extra twists to enclose the gimp must be remembered, but otherwise the honeycomb is worked in a regular way. The working of pins x and y is explained in the diagram. There can be no continuous thread between the gimps when the holes lie in a vertical position; it is possible only when the holes lie diagonally. When examined closely by the lacemaker this may appear a little odd, but it is acceptable as the obvious method to use and it is the gimps which provide the pattern effect on the headside rather than individual stitches.

49

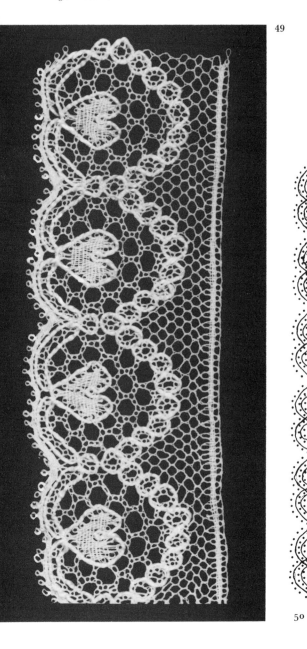

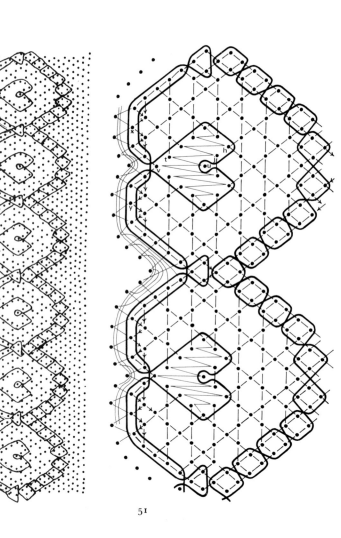

50                                    51

## EGG AND BACON

It is unlikely that this is the traditional name for this pattern; is it perhaps the 'Cucumber and Onions' referred to in Thomas Wright's *Romance of the Lace Pillow.*

(Refer to photograph 52, pricking 53 and diagram 54.) When a cloth feature lies parallel to the picot pins the cloth pins are omitted, particularly in some of the old, traditional designs. This simple pattern illustrates the method used. Set in the pattern and work the four pin buds. The pair from a, which travels out to make a picot, and the pair from the picot which will work b, cross between the buds with cloth stitch and two twists.

## The cloth and gimp threads

When the third bud has been completed, the gimps are crossed and pass through the pair from picot f and the pair from the longest row of ground. The pairs are twisted and a cloth stitch is worked. Pin h is put up between the pairs, the pin is not covered and the pairs hang as passives. The pair from picot g becomes the weaver; it travels through the headside passive pairs and is twisted twice. The gimp thread is passed between the threads of the weaver pair, which immediately works the cloth stitches through the two passive pairs. The right hand side gimp is passed through, the pair is twisted and works a ground stitch at j.

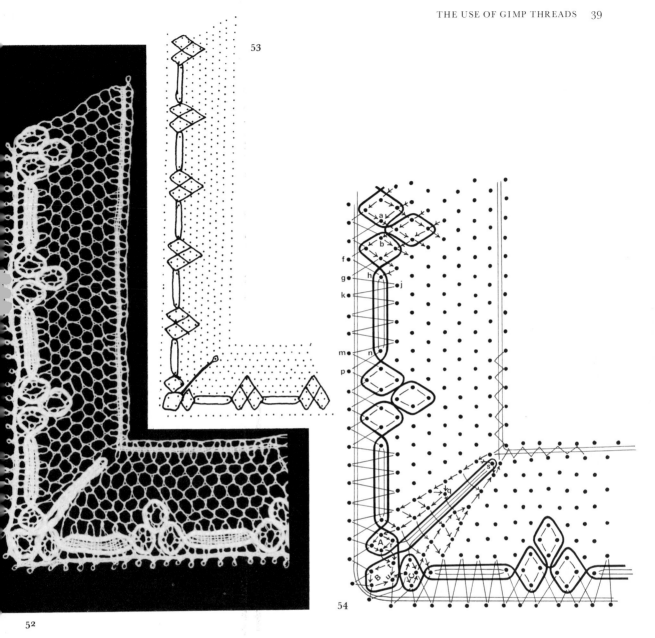

53

52

54

Pin j is put to the *left* of both pairs. The position of this pin prevents an unsightly hole between the ground and the gimp and it also improves the tension for the cloth work. The left hand pair from j is weaver; the gimp is passed through and the weaver works two cloth stitches through the passive pairs. The gimp passes between the threads of the weaver, which is then twisted twice. The weaver travels on through the passive headside pairs and works the picot at k. Work is continued in the same way to picot m. A pin is put up at n between the untwisted passive pairs, the pin is covered with a cloth stitch, and two twists are given before the gimps cross below that pin. There are no twists between the cloth and the gimps in order to increase the solidity of the feature; the twists outside the gimp threads isolate and emphasise it.

## Alternative method

This can be used for speed but it is not a traditional Bucks method; it can be used only when the passive pairs remain constant. Refer to the diagram; when the weaver has worked picot g, it travels back through the headside passive pairs and is twisted twice before the gimp. There are two gimp threads and two passive pairs – six threads in all. As no twists are given on the cloth side of the gimp, it is possible to treat these six threads as three pairs regardless of thread variation to work three cloth stitches. Three twists are given and the ground stitch for pin j is made.

*N.B.* It must be emphasised that it is unusual to use a weaver to make picots in Bucks Point lace and there are very few occasions when it is considered to be **acceptable**.

## Corner

The last ground row supplies the pair for the last ground pair of the cloth feature. There are no complete ground rows to supply the two pairs for bud A. Refer to the working diagram and select the pairs to use for the ground stitch and pin q. Work the row and the top pin of bud A. Hang one pair over the gimp to work the side pin r; complete bud A. The gimps are crossed below pin r, the right hand gimp continuing through the pair from r and through six ground pairs. These pairs remain untwisted.

The pair hanging from r works cloth stitch through all the pairs to the right and pin s is put in position; it returns through the same pairs. The gimp travels back through all these untwisted pairs, including the weaver. With the exception of the weaver all pairs are twisted three times ready for the ground. Using the principle adopted in the trefoil pattern on page 34, the gimp thread continues to the outside of the next bud. Bud B is worked beginning at pin t and finishing at pin u. The gimps are crossed for bud C. The top pin is worked with a pair from u and a picot pair. The corner weaver is used for the right side pin in the bud and then it is no longer required; it must be carried alongside the gimp and eventually discarded.

## LILLE

Certain patterns depend almost entirely on gimp for decoration. Laces of this type were often called Lille regardless of the design, perhaps because of the predominance of ground – the Lille ground. As the effect is light and uncluttered they are sometimes worked in black or in white with an ecru gimp thread. (Refer to photograph 55, pricking 56 and diagram 57.) This particular pattern gives an opportunity to consolidate various techniques described in this chapter. A fine gimp thread is recommended to emphasise the delicacy of the design. There are two passive pairs on the headside between the gimp and the picots throughout.

## To begin

It can be started along the diagonal ground row which ends at pin A. Alternatively the ground can be set in along a horizontal row from pin B. To begin it is necessary to have one pair available from each of A, B and C and two pairs from E. Hang three gimp threads on pin D; two threads are required for the right hand side and one to travel along the headside. Using one pair from E and one from A work the ground stitch and put up a pin at a. Using the second pair on E work the ground stitch and put up pin b. Take the left hand pair round the gimp, twist it twice and work through two passive pairs hung on a support pin behind the work; make a picot at c. The picot pair returns through the two passive pairs in cloth stitch, is twisted and passes round the gimp. Three more twists are required for the ground. The next ground row, d, e, and f is worked but the pin at f is treated as a catch pin; pin f is put to the left of both pairs. This technique was used in the previous pattern. The picot is worked and a third row of ground from C.

## Honeycomb rings

The gimps are separated for the rings which are worked in the usual way. At the bottom of the second ring the gimp threads are crossed and the one no longer required passes through two pairs from the ring to the right of centre. It lies back across the work to be cut off later. Similarly, another gimp is taken back through the gimp for firmness and laid back to be cut off later in the ring which is close to the headside. At points M, N, and O some attention to thread arrangement is required. There appears to be one picot hole missing but as the hole arrangement is even and the pattern is otherwise good, it is preferable to solve the problem with unobtrusive use of threads rather than introduce an alteration to the pattern. It is an old pattern, well used and should be worked without difficulty. If one pair is temporarily placed alongside the gimp the problem

55

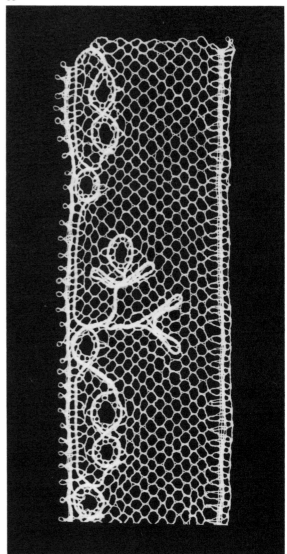

is solved. The pair from n is used for the picot as it maintains the diagonal line of working; the pair from m would cause a hole and weak area.

## Gimp fingers

A new gimp pair is required for the ring P. The use of gimp for the fingers is clarified in the diagram. One gimp thread is used for both fingers; the gimps should lie crossed and together at the bottom of the ring. Diagonal rows of ground are worked below the ring on either side. The pair from o passes round two gimp threads to work a ground stitch at p. The left hand gimp passes to the left through the pairs necessary to work ground stitch and pin q. The two pairs through the gimp remain untwisted and the right hand pair from q works through them in cloth stitch. The gimp travels to the right through the two pairs and the

weaver; these pairs are untwisted. It travels on to the right through four pairs more; a ground stitch is worked and pin r is put up. The left hand pair from r works cloth stitch through untwisted pairs from o and p. The gimp travels to the left through one pair from r, the untwisted cloth pairs from o and p, the untwisted weaver. The pair from q is already round one gimp thread but must pass round two more. Thus the pairs from q and r meet to the right of all the gimp threads. They must be twisted three times; a ground stitch is worked and pin s put in position. Pin s must be very firm to hold the gimp threads and maintain good tension. A soft pillow, an old pricking with large holes or the use of bent pins will spoil the design.

The ground must be worked to t and u before the remaining fingers are worked. The gimp travels through both pairs at t and u and through six pairs more in order to

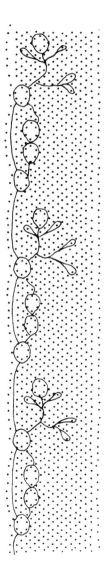

56

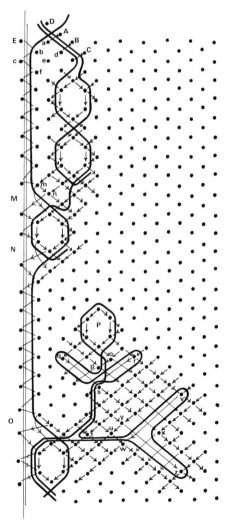

57

work the ground stitch and pin v. The left hand pair from v works through three untwisted pairs in cloth stitch and is left hanging for use later. The gimp is brought back through the pair at v and three cloth pairs. The row of ground can be worked to x. Three more rows of ground are worked. The gimp is taken through the pair from x and on through three pairs more. The pair from y which hangs round the gimp works four cloth stitches towards z. The weaver and the last pair taken through the gimp are twisted three times, a ground stitch is made and pin z is put up. The gimp travels back through to the left through all pairs except for the headside passives. Refer to the diagram. All pairs are twisted and ground worked, beginning with the stitch and pin w. This is similar to the pattern on page 37. These fingers give the pattern solidity; there are no twists inside the gimp fingers but they are emphasised by the twists outside.

## A PATTERN TO SHOW GIMP FINGERS IN HONEYCOMB

If all the honeycomb holes are present the method is straightforward; when holes are omitted the pattern is treated differently from ground, where the emphasis is on solidity. In honeycomb the stitches are used to fix the gimp in the required position; a study of the holes usually suggests a use of threads. (Refer to photograph 58, pricking 59 and diagram 60.) The arrangement of the one pair of gimp threads required is logical but may at first appear complicated. There are three pinholes missing in the honeycomb and pairs fall into the vertical rows as shown in the diagram. The gimp thread provides strength on the diagonal. The honeycomb should be worked from left to right, i.e. from the head down to the footside. When the honeycomb is complete the left gimp is crossed by the right and travels on until the ground stitch is worked and pin a is in position. The left hand pair from pin a works four cloth stitches and the ground stitch at b. The gimps cross below pin b. The headside is worked from picot c to picot d; it should be worked at this stage in its entirety. The headside pairs are ready for the finger in the ground and the honeycomb. Work as many ground stitches as possible; bring the crossed gimp down to include the pair required for f. Using one passive pair from the headside and the first ground pair work a ground stitch and pin e. The right hand pair makes four cloth stitches and is used for the ground stitch at f. The gimp travels back to e and the pairs cross ready for the honeycomb.

### Corner

Four extra pairs make two false picots. Only three pairs are actually used, but the general appearance of the lace is improved by the use of the false picot rather than by the casual introduction of one pair over a gimp thread, which may distort it. As the last complete pattern before the corner is worked, the ground is worked and left along a horizontal line as shown in the diagram. At position o there is no hole but the left hand catch pin pair and the pair to the left of it make a ground stitch to fill the space and allow the pairs to fall naturally in the correct direction. The

ground stitch at g is worked using one inner passive pair and the right hand pair from position o. When the pin is in position the left of these pairs works five cloth stitches to the ground stitch and pin h. At this stage the headside picots can be worked all together. The honeycomb stitches are worked from pin j. With the addition of the false picots there are sufficient pairs to complete the honeycomb at k. The gimp threads cross and one travels back to the corner at n. The inner passive pair and right hand pair from k work a

58

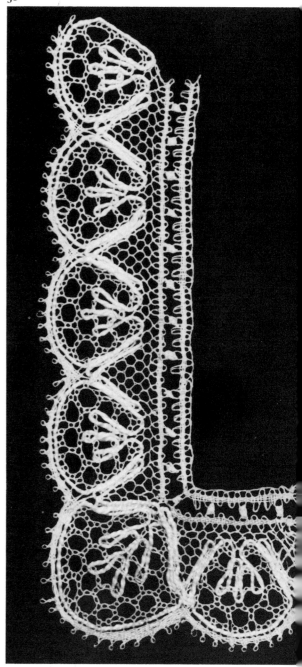

ground stitch and pin m is put up. The right hand pair from m works five cloth stitches and makes a cloth stitch with the pair from x. The gimp thread returns towards the head and the right hand pair from n becomes the inner passive. The left hand pair from n crosses the corner pair from the honeycomb at position p without a pin and is used for the catch pin stitch. The ground is worked, the first set of holes being along a horizontal line. The corner and thread used on either side is symmetrical. The picot pins are worked and the extra pairs discarded from the headside passives.

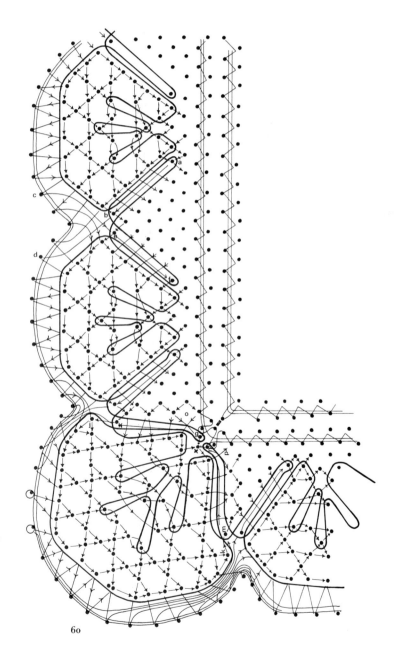

59

60

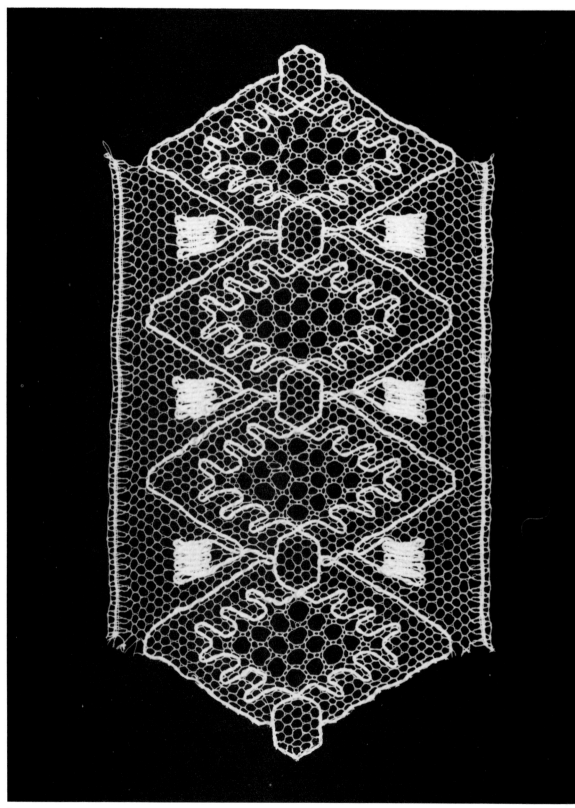

# INSERTION

This pattern is one of a group that was made in the Hampden and Princes Risborough area of mid-Buckinghamshire at the end of the nineteenth century. Others made in the same villages are on pages 52 and 128. This particular pattern has unusual use of gimp thread in the ground. From a distance the separate gimp threads in the square block cannot be distinguished, but give a shiny 'cushioned' effect. The pairs travel vertically holding the gimp thread, which is kept taut by pins at either side. As in the previous pattern the gimp thread moving in a horizontal direction maintains the tension of the lace. (Refer to photograph 61, pricking 62.) The arrangement of holes is very regular and the working of the lace straightforward. There is one gimp pair to outline the diamond shape and work the gimp feature in the ground. The other gimp pair emphasises the honeycomb and the central hexagon. The three stitches within the fingers extending into the ground may be worked in ground or honeycomb according to the wishes of the lacemaker; if honeycomb stitch is chosen it will extend the honeycomb effect and make the lace appear firm and close.

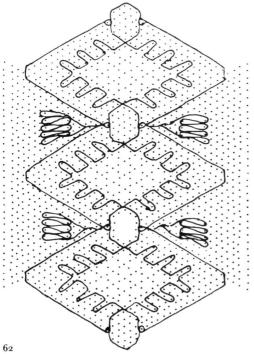

62

# A FLORAL PATTERN

Taken and extended from a small draft, the corner was added and centre reversal placed. (Refer to the photograph 63, pricking 64 and diagram 65.) At first sight the pattern appears to be regular and straightforward to work, but there are several unexpected problems. The working diagram suggests ways of dealing with the situations, but there are many possibilities. The important consideration is the appearance and the strength of the finished lace. Many of the techniques already discussed in this chapter are used here; some require adaptation and others are used in a different situation. For example, honeycomb pins between passive headside pairs and the pattern feature appeared in the pattern on page 37; in this pattern there is no enclosing gimp and the pairs come from cloth, but the method is similar. However, to maintain a piece of cloth with good tension, cloth stitch with two twists may be worked before the pin and a normal honeycomb stitch after the pin. This does not distort the honeycomb but provides better tension for the weaver. This method can be used inside the honeycomb shape when required. The other pins are put into position to support the weaver on the honeycomb side of the gimp; the weaver is twisted and travels back round the gimps and passive pairs.

One method of working the cloth is shown. There are alternative ways; but the chief problem is to keep the ground regular with the odd number of holes given. If a pair is brought round the gimp thread and a ground stitch worked at position v, the ground can be worked normally. There is no need to put up a pin at v, therefore it is unnecessary to alter or modify the original pattern. In many elaborate patterns it becomes necessary to work stitches without pinholes to maintain good tension and appearance; their omission is deliberate as pinholes very close together cause confusion and may be inaccurate. In the diagram the double arrow, in blue, indicates the addition of two pairs to fall either side of the gimp. (Refer to page 117.) The single arrowed line indicates that a pair is carried with the gimp until required. The short lines indicate pairs that have no further use; they are carried with the gimp and discarded.

# NOOK PINS

To ensure that a gimp thread remains close to the outline of the design it is necessary to hold it in indentations using the weaver and a pin. This pin is known as the nook pin. The method of working depends entirely on the complexity of the design and the position of the pin within the half stitch or cloth feature. The use of gimp and pin must be examined in the context of one particular situation only; the aim is to hold the gimp thread firmly but unobtrusively. When a gimp thread extends into ground or honeycomb it becomes obvious which pairs come to the pin to make the stitch. Similarly, the nook pin holds the most convenient pair or pairs available. There are many ways of achieving the desired result, that is, a smooth cloth feature with no interruption in the flow of the passive pairs. Various situations are discussed in the next two patterns.

65

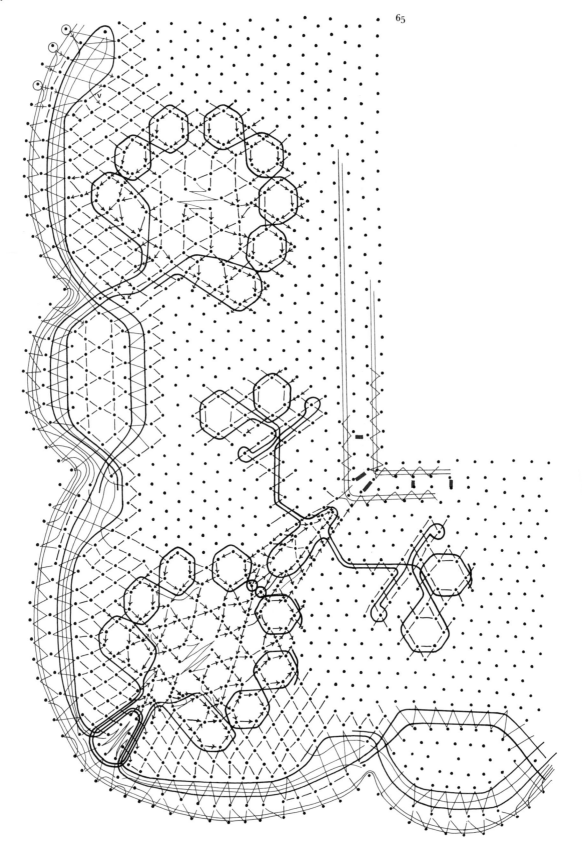

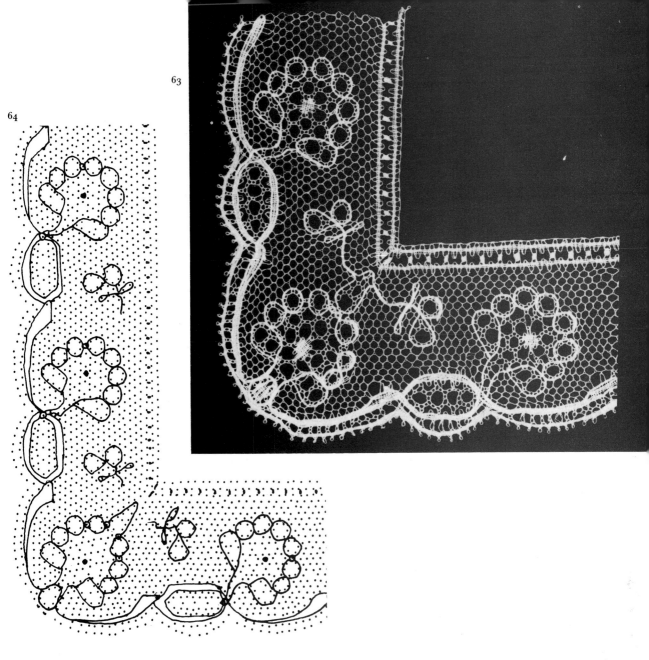

**64**

**63**

## HEART AND RINGS

This is one of many patterns where the cloth is broken by the gimp thread; it shows the basic method of working the most common nook pin. (Refer to photograph 66, pricking 67 and diagram 68.) The pattern is regular; honeycomb rings A and B are completed and the row of ground to c. The gimps are crossed and the right hand gimp thread travels through both pairs from c and on through the next seven pairs for the heart. The diagram indicates the working of the cloth heart. The weaver from n travels to the right through the three pairs within the heart, and remains untwisted; the gimp is passed through and the weaver is twisted three times. A ground stitch is made and catch pin p is put up to the left of both pairs. The weaver continues to s.

## Nook pin

A decision must be reached regarding the availability of pairs for the nook pin. Nook pin t falls exactly below the top centre pin, therefore the pair from that pin falls vertically to work the stitch at that pin. The pair at r will be required for w but moves to the right to work ground pin v before returning to the cloth heart and pin w. The weaver at s travels to the right through three cloth pairs. The gimp thread is brought through the pair at r and .through the pair which hangs vertically in the cloth from the top centre pin. Both pairs are twisted twice before the gimp is passed through. The gimp passes through the next pair which is the heart weaver; no twists are given to the weaver before the gimp is passed through. The weaver and vertical pair are twisted twice to enclose the gimp, a cloth stitch is worked and the pin put in at t. It is covered, the pairs receive two twists each and the gimp travels back to the right through these pairs which return to normal working. The left hand weaver pair is untwisted, and it works back to the left through four cloth pairs to the point of the heart at u. It returns to the right through six pairs (i.e. four pairs hanging in the cloth, one pair from nook pin t which must be twisted twice, and one pair from ground stitch v). This pair is brought round the gimp and twisted twice before it becomes part of the cloth heart. Pin x is worked as pin p. It is usual to omit twists on the weaver between cloth and gimp but to twist elsewhere as appropriate.

66

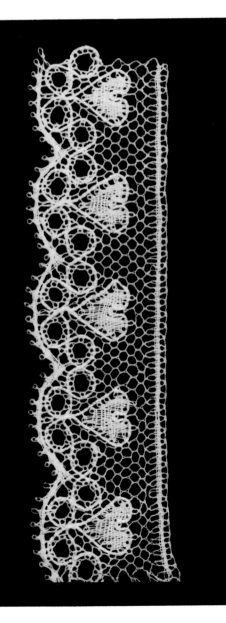

67

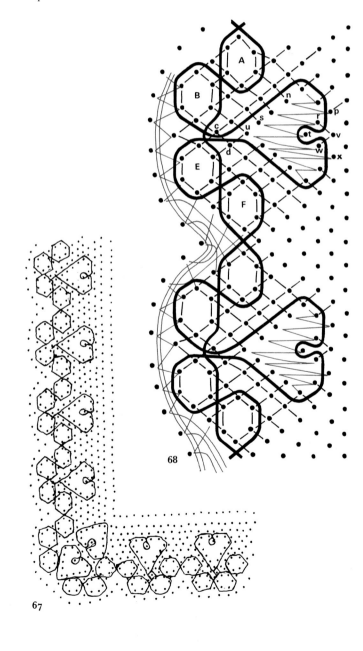

68

## Gimp thread

This encloses the heart and crosses the other gimp thread. There are no twists between gimp threads; twists made in preparation for the ground stitch at d hold them closely together. A row of ground stitches is worked diagonally below the heart from d. Honeycomb rings E and F are worked. The stitches between rings and picots are worked in honeycomb. A corner can be worked using pricking 90.

## GRETCHEN

In the North Bucks Lace Association catalogue this lace pattern is labelled 'Gretchen'; it was offered for sale at 10s. 6d. per yard ($52\frac{1}{2}$p) in 1900. To earn 10s. 6d. in one week the lacemaker had to work two complete pattern repeats every day and this does not include the time taken to wind the bobbins, nor the cost of the thread! (Refer to photograph 69, pricking 70 and diagrams 71, 72 and 73.)

This pattern is typical of many Bucks Point patterns where the weaver is used at nook pins to hold the gimp thread close to the cloth design. Each situation is different but a variety are discussed here; ultimately the decision is made at the discretion of the lacemaker.

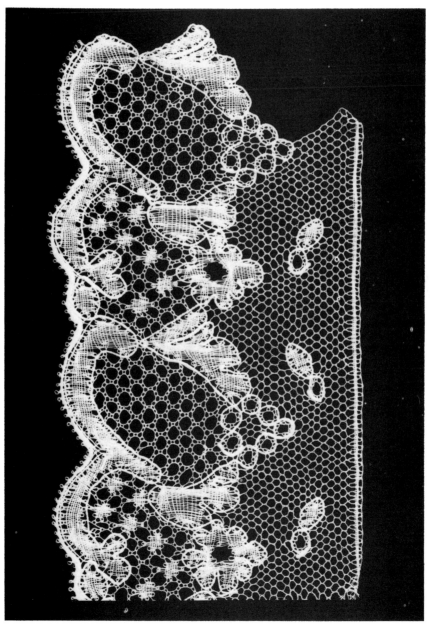

69

## Nook pins at A

(Refer to diagram 71 and position A on the pricking 70.)
*Pin b.* The weaver at a works cloth stitch to the right through four pairs and the gimp from the right passes through the weaver pair which is untwisted. Pin b is put up between the weaver and the gimp thread. The weaver is twisted twice and the gimp thread passes back through the weaver pair and on through the pairs for cloth beginning at pin c. The pair at b loses its function as a weaver, is twisted twice and becomes a passive pair in cloth to fill any space which could occur below b. Two pairs work a cloth stitch and pin c is put up; a new weaver continues to work the cloth stitch. Pin d is discussed below, but in order to understand the nook pin at b, note that the weaver from d travels with cloth stitch through all the pairs to e. The pair from b is part of the cloth and as the cloth stitch tension is maintained it will keep the gimp in the correct position.
*Pin d.* This pin is worked similarly to the nook pin in the previous pattern. The weaver travels towards the nook pin, as far as but not through the pair hanging directly above it. This vertical cloth pair is twisted twice, the gimp is brought from the right through this pair and through the untwisted weaver pair. The weaver and vertical pair are twisted and a cloth stitch is worked. Pin d is put up and covered with another cloth stitch. Both pairs are twisted twice and the gimp returns to the right hand side. The weaver remains untwisted and the passive cloth pair (the right hand pair) is twisted twice and hangs below nook pin d to fill the space and become part of the cloth. The weaver works to e and back to position f; it works cloth through the pair from d and waits in that position to work f later. As pin g is above f it is necessary to begin the cloth at g with new pairs. One pair will come from the ground and the other from the cloth above and to the left of g. When pin g has been covered the weaver works to the right to h and then back to position f. It is important to work to h to keep h, f and e on a horizontal line; this prevents holes in the cloth and ensures better tension. The two weavers meet at f, work a cloth stitch, pin f is put between them, and another cloth stitch is made to cover the pin. One pair continues to weave and the other becomes a passive to fill the space below f. In this situation the weaver worked to the left; the decision was reached after counting the holes to the next nook pin. To work a nook pin the weaver must travel across the cloth to the pin in the normal sequence using pin holes on either side alternately, in this pattern from j to k.
*Pin k.* The weaver from j works to the right as far as but not through the pair hanging vertically above pin k. The weaver remains untwisted but the vertical cloth pair is twisted twice. The gimp comes from the right to the left through pairs including the weaver; the weaver and vertical pair are twisted, a cloth stitch is made and the nook pin k is put up. Cloth stitch is worked to cover the pin and both pairs are twisted twice. The weaver passes round the gimp and untwisted works back to m. The gimp passes through the pair from k and on through pairs hanging down from the previous cloth. It is unnecessary to twist between the gimps unless a particular effect is required. Before weaving is recommenced the gimp is enclosed with twists. As the pin hole at n is no higher than the nook pin k

it is satisfactory to continue with the same weaver to o. Pinhole n is ignored and pairs allowed to fall into the cloth over a gimp. The weaver 'absorbs' them into the cloth and the work lies flat.

## Nook pin at B

(Refer to diagram 72 and position B on the pricking 70.)
*Pin p.* Two considerations arise when selecting the pair to work with the weaver at nook pin p. As previously, the chief consideration is to choose the pair hanging vertically above the pin. It is advantageous to assess the number of pairs required to complete the cloth which extends to the right and to work out the use of pairs in the honeycomb. The wider the area of cloth and the farther the nook pin is inside the cloth, the more choice there can be. When the use of pairs has been decided, the weaver works to pin q and on to pin r. In a regular diamond shape with six pin hole the position and pair for dividing to two separate cloth areas is obvious. (Refer to page 139.) In this pattern the method is the same but the choice of passive pair for the top pin has to be assessed by counting the threads required for each section of the pattern.

## Nook pins at C

(Refer to diagram 73 and position C on the pricking 70.)
*Pin s.* This is worked in the same way as pin k. Another point of interest arises here. The pins at the top of the cloth lie on a horizontal line. The weaver works to t and across to u. Pin u and pin v are on the same horizontal line and the weaver travels from u to v ignoring all the pins along the top. The honeycomb above the cloth is incomplete at o. However, it is usual to work the appropriate pairs together at position o so that they fall evenly into the cloth below. Some lacemakers like to put pins into the holes to steady the pairs, but no stitches are made and provided that the lacemaker pulls the pairs to the correct position this is not really necessary. When the pairs have been brought from the honeycomb through the gimp to be 'absorbed' into the cloth do they require twisting to enclose the gimp? A close study of old lace will reveal no definite rule. Sometimes twists were given, but quite often they were missed out. As some well made lace lacks the twists one cannot assume that it was through carelessness. It is more likely that, after careful consideration of the overall effect within the design, the lacemaker decided to omit them. Some people will argue that gimps are always enclosed, whilst others regard the appearance as more important. In the pattern on page 38 the twists on the weaver were omitted to give a solid effect. If the twists are omitted on the passive pairs in this pattern the cloth will appear solid. However, the gimp will become less obvious and its function is to outline and enhance the design. Either method is acceptable and must remain the decision of the lacemaker.
*Pin w.* At pin x consideration must be given to the need for pairs to complete the cloth on the right, and to note which pair falls above the nook pin w. The weaver from x works to y as far as but not including the pair over nook pin w. The weaver completes the cloth on the right. The gimp thread moves to the left through the pairs from the cloth and through the pair hanging vertically above w. It is

twisted before and after the gimp. Pin w is put up between the gimp and the new weaver. The gimp passes back through the weaver; thus pin w is enclosed by gimp but no stitch. The pair hanging at w becomes the new weaver to complete the cloth. It is important to ensure that a passive pair will fall below the nook pin to prevent a hole from forming. In this pattern a pair is available from y. However, if no pair is available the appearance of the finished lace is improved if an extra pair is joined in at y.

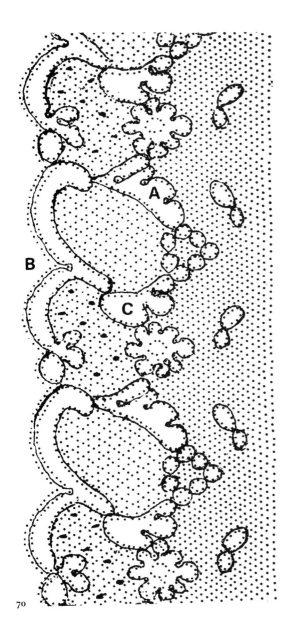

70

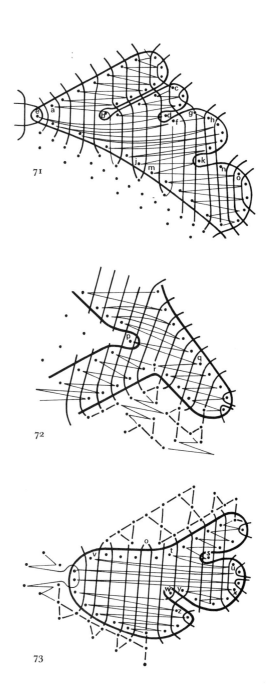

71

72

73

## AN OLD BUCKS POINT PATTERN

This pricking came from the Hampden and Princes
Risborough area. (Refer to pricking 74.) It is interesting to
note that the ground near the footside and the ground
within the pattern are different, although at the same angle
the ground within the pattern has the holes closer together.
The ground has been pricked across the corner; lines to the
sides of the pricking indicate the footside equivalent and
the direction of working. (Refer to Chapter 4.)

74

# 4 Corners

The designing and working of corners for straight edgings is a challenge. In the past very few patterns had corners as lace was worked by the length round a pillow. Most of the corners for the narrow, traditional edgings have been designed within the last 30 years to satisfy the demands of the modern lacemaker. To work a corner successfully it is necessary to understand the construction. To design a corner it is essential to understand the principles of pattern making. Chapters 5 and 9 explain this in detail.

## GENERAL POINTS TO CONSIDER WHEN DESIGNING A CORNER

As all Bucks Point patterns are worked along a diagonal line at an angle of 52° or more from the footside, some adaptations of the design must be made or a new idea superimposed across the corner. Only in Torchon lace is it possible to cut a pricking along the 45° line, turn the pillow and continue the lace.

To investigate the possible corner designs, take a straight-edged mirror and move it along the pricking at an angle of 45°. The wider patterns with floral designs can be adapted more easily than the narrow geometric edgings.

(Refer to diagram 75.) When making any edging the directions for working ground or honeycomb are shown by the arrows at a. The pattern may be worked to line x; the arrow on the diagram shows the direction of working. When the corner is complete and the pillow turned, work continues down the diagonal line y in the direction indicated. Ground and honeycomb may be worked in the directions shown by the arrows at b. It is not possible to change direction across the corner line z, and therefore a new feature must be introduced to separate the two areas of ground, before and after the corner. This can be solid as in the pattern on page 38, but it is more usual to make a design feature with a honeycomb or ground filling in the centre. Everything within the shaded area is worked at a different angle. Line z is the corner line and C is the position of the footside for the corner area. As the corner extends from one corner pin, there can be only one footside pin on line C. In future this line is known as the footside equivalent. The blue arrows in this area indicate the direction of working ground and honeycomb. A selection of edgings with corners will be used to explain the method of making the corner and the way in which it is worked. It is essential to consider the working method when planning the design and arrangement of the holes.

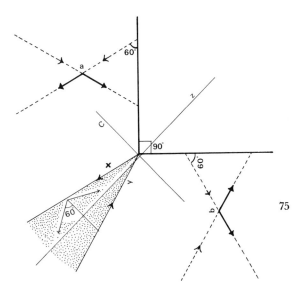

75

## DOUBLE RING PATTERN

Refer to diagram 76(a), (b) and (c). Place a mirror on diagram 76(a); when it lies on the corner line the gap is hardly noticeable. This is because the edging is very narrow and is worked at an angle of 51° from the footside. Rule a line through a footside hole at 45° across the corner. Prick two or more copies of the edging as shown in 76(a). The last complete row of ground is included, the corner pin and both honeycomb rings. As the picots may need adjustment the last three are not pricked. Finally prick in two holes beyond the pattern to indicate the position of the 45° line. On the top copy mark in the gimp lines. Turn the second copy over and mark in the gimp lines as in diagram 76(b). (The second copy is marked on the rough underside of the pricking.) On one piece scratch a straight line across the corner through the corner pin and balance marks. Fold the excess paper underneath by creasing along the scratch line; this is quicker and more accurate than cutting the paper. Also, should it be necessary to adopt another idea, the pricking can be flattened and refolded. Working on a pricking board, take the two paper prickings, and match the corner pin and two holes beyond the pattern. Placing pins well out of the pricking area fasten the prickings together. Check that the corner is a right angle and decide how to fill the space. The rings on the headside are close enough for the gimp to be continuous, and the threads will pass from one ring to the next without difficulty. (Refer to diagram 76(c).) If a honeycomb ring is placed across the centre, the central space will be no larger than a ring and therefore acceptable. The three honeycomb holes (in blue) are added and four picot pins. The purpose of these pins will be seen when the working diagram 79 is studied and the lace is made.

### To work the corner

(Refer to photograph 77, pricking 78 and diagram 79.) It is necessary to complete the diagonal from v before working ring a. Introduce a new gimp through the pairs required for pins 1, 2 and 3. When deciding which pairs are needed, consider them as ground pins and the choice is obvious. The right hand pair for pin 1 comes from the catch pin w and the pair for 3 comes from the inner passive pair. Using honeycomb, work pins 1, 2 and 3 in the ring. Work ring a completely. Work pin 4 in preparation for ring e. The pair marked with an asterisk cannot be used for ring b and is carried with the gimp until required for ring e. Care should be taken to ensure that it *remains with the gimp* and does not cross the centre space. Rings b, d and e are worked. A pair from the point of e passes round both gimp threads to work pin 5. Pin 6 is put up and enclosed with a honeycomb stitch using the pairs from pin 3. The ring is completed at pin 7; the gimps overlap and are discarded. The pair from pin 6 again becomes the inner passive.

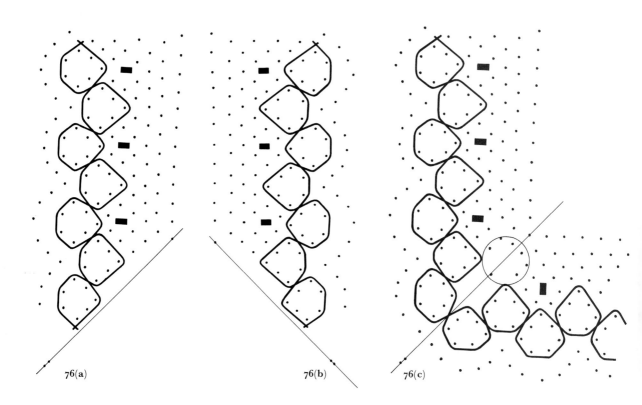

76(a)                    76(b)                    76(c)

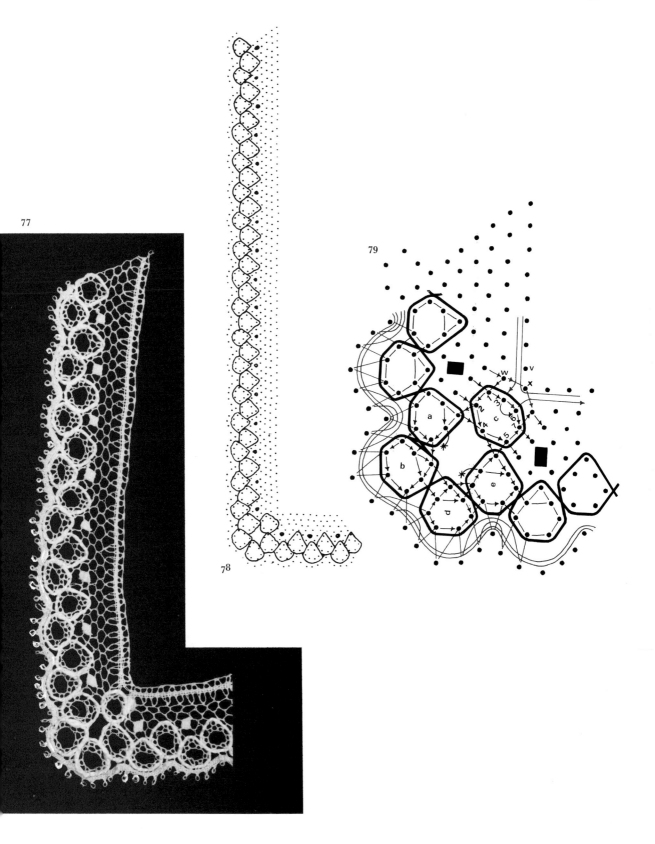

77

78

79

## HONEYCOMB AND DIAMOND PATTERN

(Refer to photograph 80, pricking 81 and diagram 82.)
Most of the narrow patterns are made at an angle not
exceeding 55° from the footside, therefore the space in the
corner can be fairly small. For convenience rather than
beauty many patterns are arranged with a narrow area of
honeycomb extending from the footside to the picots.
Several of the patterns in Chapter 2 have corners arranged
in this way, but it is successful only if the honeycomb can
echo a honeycomb feature in the pattern. To work out the
corner pricking it is necessary to mark in the line across the
corner, also to draw in lines parallel to the footsides along
the outside of the curve. Extended, these will indicate the
position of the picots at the corner. It is important to
achieve a square corner on the headside; the pattern on
page 58 does not make a good corner as it is too rounded at

the picot position. The pins along the gap row in the
corner honeycomb should lie on the corner line. The
diagram explains the working method. It is necessary to
add three pairs on the headside, and two false picots are
made and the extra pair discarded in the headside passives.
The honeycomb is started at pin F and completed at pin G.
At X there is one pair too many to work a honeycomb
stitch and pin. The honeycomb pair travelling to the
corner works through the extra pair in cloth stitch and two
twists before pin X is worked with the pair from the corner
pin. The right hand pair at this pin goes back to work the
corner pin a second time. The left hand pair, which
continues the honeycomb, works through the extra pair
with cloth stitch and two twists before working the
honeycomb pins back to G.

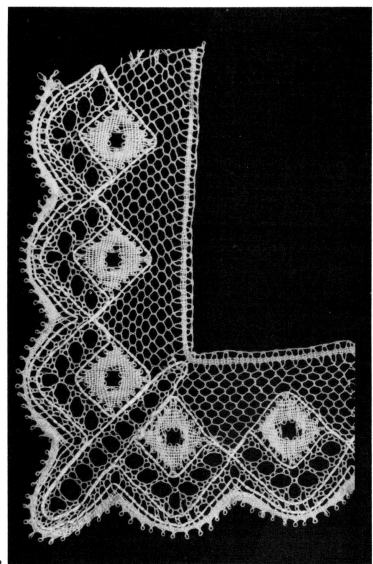

80

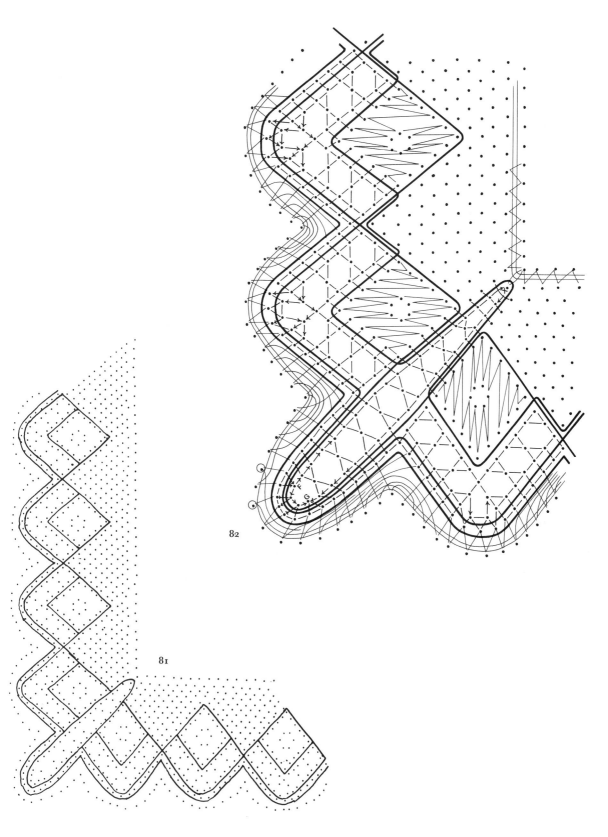

82

81

## A PATTERN USING THE DESIGN ACROSS THE CORNER

Another method of making a neat corner is to use the design across the corner. (Refer to photograph 83, pricking 84 and diagram 85.) It is usually necessary to increase the size of the corner motif and consequently to replan the holes. Use a mirror on the pricking to assess the space required for the corner motif. Mark in the corner diagonal from a foot pin. Prick and join the pricking as described in the first pattern. Draw the corner motif in freely. Take a piece of clear, rigid plastic and prick onto it a grid for honeycomb, the same size as on this pattern. Mark the footside equivalent and a line at 90° through the points of the honeycomb diamonds. Match this line with the corner

diagonal and the heart shape can be pricked into the corner. The honeycomb within the side oval shapes is added by eye to use to best advantage pairs from the ground and to provide pairs for the central honeycomb feature. The holes in the ring are based on the ground holes either side of the corner. It must be emphasised that this takes considerable time and often several attempts before a satisfactory corner is achieved. Compare this corner with the next pattern. In this pattern the design reduces the width of the space at the corner, which is very rounded. The next pattern has a corner which extends out to the normal picot line; this is more attractive but more difficult to manage. The diagram explains the working method; no additional pairs are necessary.

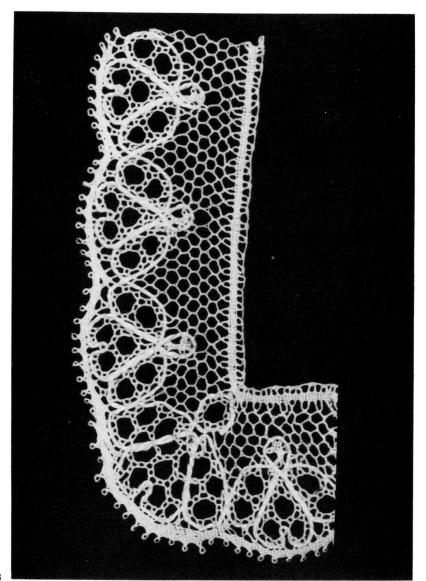

83

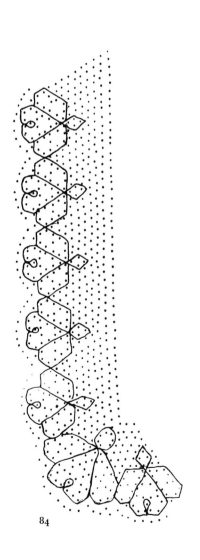

84

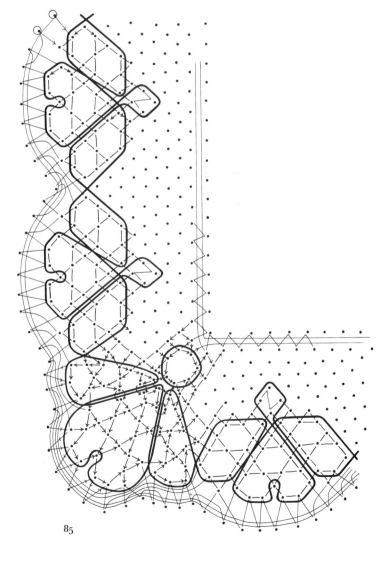

85

## A SECOND PATTERN USING AN EXTENDED DESIGN ACROSS THE CORNER

(Refer to photograph 86 and pricking 87.) The same method of preparing a pricking is adopted for this pattern. To avoid a rounded corner the design was extended to include extra diamonds and honeycomb. The motif was planned on clear plastic film as described in the previous pattern. If the edging has a cucumber foot, it is essential that the inner passive pairs should remain straight and enter the centre feature; in this case they are used to provide the pairs for the honeycomb within the ring. As the distance between picots and gimp is greater than usual on the headside, honeycomb stitches and pins are used to fill the gap and to improve the tension. The holes across the bottom of the honeycomb bear no relation to the holes in the ground, therefore the available pairs should be used to achieve neatness and strength. The use of the pairs, particularly at the centre ground hole, is unorthodox but satisfactory. Diagram 88 clarifies the method of working.

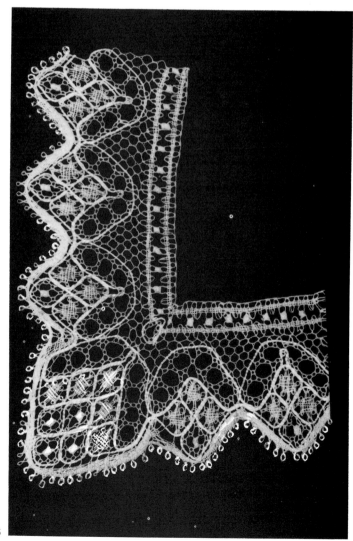

86

87

88

## A THIRD PATTERN USING THE FEATURE
## ACROSS THE CORNER

(Refer to photograph 89, pricking 90 and diagram 91.) To
fill the corner and to make a break in the ground, the heart
is set in as shown in the diagram. A grid pricked onto
clear plastic was used as described for previous patterns.
Many narrow edgings do not offer many possibilities for
corner design; however, this arrangement allows the lace
to be used for handkerchiefs. Extra pairs are added as
shown by blue arrows. When no longer required they are
carried with the gimp thread until secure. Short blue lines
indicate these pairs.

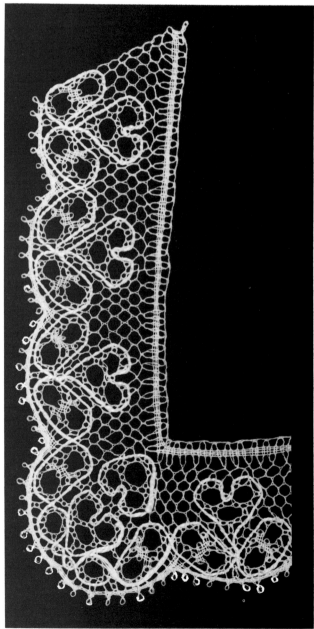

89

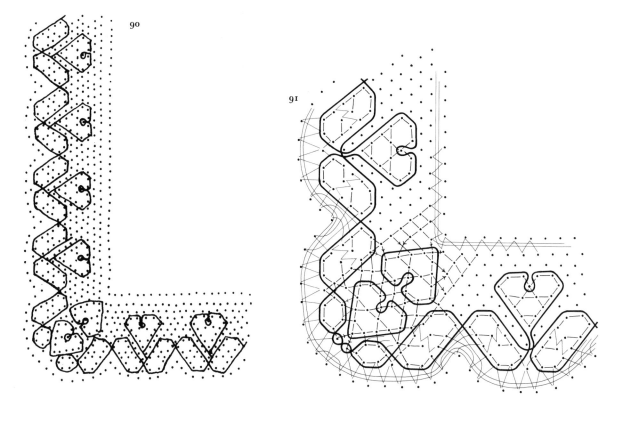

## FLORAL PATTERN

This pattern was pricked from an old draft at Luton
Museum. The draft consisted of one repeat, two flowers at
the head and the cluster of cloth and honeycomb rings. It is
unnecessary to reverse the pattern at the corner if a suitable
design to effect continuity can be made. The position of the
pattern features was altered and arranged so that there was
a complete break in the ground across the corner. (Refer to
the photograph 92, pricking 93 and diagram 94.) The
diagram indicates the direction in which the ground is
worked and it also shows the weaver for the cloth petals.
The making of this piece of lace requires considerable skill
and knowledge, but the corner presents no additional
problems.

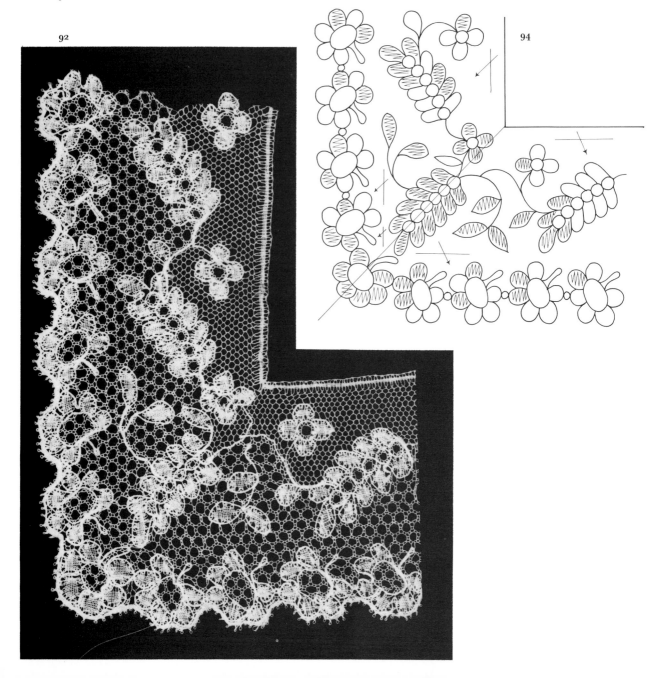

92

94

## SUMMARY OF THE IMPORTANT POINTS TO CONSIDER WHEN DESIGNING CORNERS

1. The finished lace must be strong and there must be adequate links between the various features and the ground.

2. The design should be pleasing and related to the design features of the edging.

3. The design should be extended to the outside so that the picot edge is almost at an angle of 90°.

4. The break in the ground must be complete.

5. Any ground or honeycomb within the corner area must be pricked across the corner. Other fillings used must be pricked similarly.

## SUMMARY OF THE IMPORTANT POINTS TO APPLY WHEN WORKING CORNERS

1. Study the pricking carefully to find out how the ground and/or honeycomb has been pricked and in order to be certain of the direction of working.

2. Always work as far as possible along the edging before beginning to work the corner. In this way the lacemaker understands which pairs are available and the direction in which they are travelling.

3. Assess the availability of pairs. Never drag pairs out of line or in the wrong direction as holes will appear and the tension of the lace will be lost.

4. If there are no available pairs, extra pairs must be added to work the design and maintain a strong and durable piece of lace. It is important that these pairs link the pattern features. For example, a pair required for a ground stitch must be added in the adjacent pattern feature so that it enters the ground diagonally and actually joins the two areas.

5. The weaver maintains a horizontal position and the passive pairs are vertical when working a straight edging. As the corner is worked the weaver and the passive pairs should remain in the same working positions. Occasionally it is difficult to achieve this and the cloth is worked with a diagonal weaver; the lacemaker has to make the decision in which the appearance and ease of working are the guiding factors.

93

96

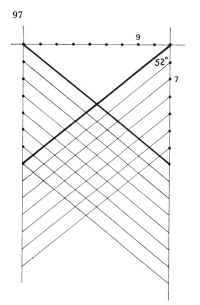

**4 5**

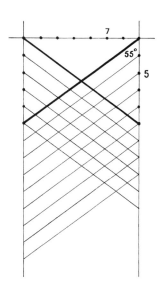

**55**

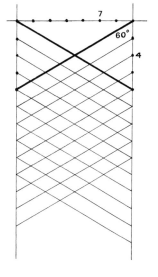

**6 0**

97

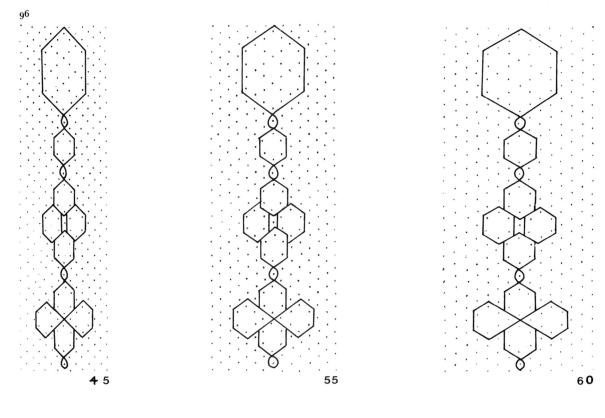

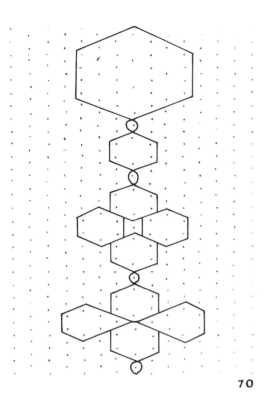

**70**

2. Some old patterns have very accurate ground. The pattern may be used as a template, the clear plastic sheet placed *underneath* and a good copy made. The two old prickings, 99, can be used in this way. However, the book provides only the paper reproduction and a copy can be made from this.

3. Photocopies of old prickings or grids as dots on white paper are sometimes available, and these require careful pricking to achieve an accurate grid. This is discussed fully in the next chapter (page 80). Grids are given on pages 160 and 163.

## TO PLOT THE FOOTSIDE HOLES ON A GROUND PRICKING

(Refer back to diagram 98.) The distance between the catch pin row and the footside is greater than the distance between the other rows to accommodate the two passive pairs. The footside holes are indicated in blue; they replace the ground holes ringed in black. Note that they are positioned on a level with the ground holes they replace. Consequently the footside pin holes are *not* on the diagonal line of the ground holes.

## THE PREPARATION OF A GRID FOR USE IN BUCKS POINT LACE

The lacemaker who wishes to design patterns or adapt old ones must collect a set of accurate grids pricked onto clear vellum or tough plastic film. Each one should be labelled with the footside line and the direction of working; the angle must also be clearly indicated. These grids are acquired in a variety of ways:

1. Grids at various angles may be drawn up. (Refer to diagram 97.) For the majority of lacemakers who are unaccustomed to this type of work, it is easier to use a normal graph paper with 8 squares to the inch (25mm) than to attempt to mark even divisions on a straight line. Using a pencil with a sharp point, draw in the Bucks Point grid lines; the intersections of the pencil lines are the positions of the holes for point ground. (Refer to diagram 98.) The grid achieved has holes that are $\frac{1}{8}$in (3mm) apart. It will be too coarse for Bucks Point patterns, but it has the advantage of accuracy over a finer grid. Many of the shops which specialise in photocopying will reduce the grid as required. Alternatively the grid may be pricked onto plain white cartridge paper. The pricking must have a black paper behind it, and it can be photocopied, or photocopied and reduced, as before.

98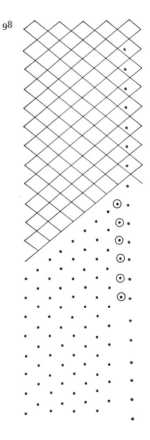

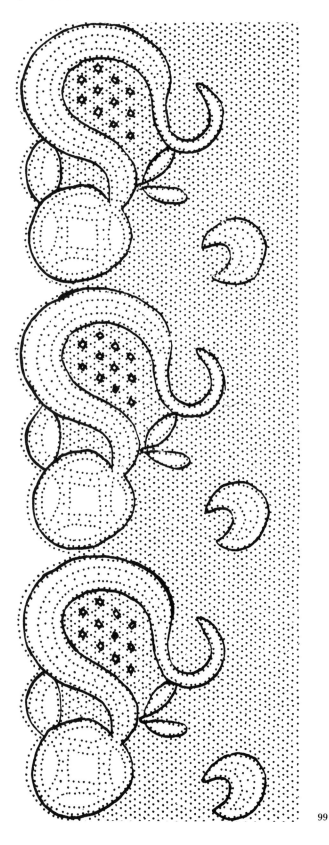

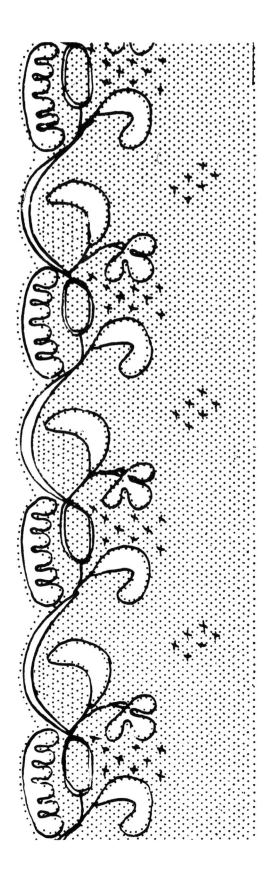

## TO WORK FOOTSIDE AND GROUND

In the eighteenth century many workers made the lace without using ground pins. Old patterns exist with two rows of holes on the footside, holes indicating some design features and the picot holes on the outside edge. The tension and accuracy depended on the rhythmic movement of bobbins and the resultant speed. With practice any lacemaker can feel the taut thread that travels along the diagonal row. Working from right to left, the travelling thread remains on the left of the four bobbins as each ground stitch is completed. Thus, at the end of a row of ground, the end thread has travelled from the footside and maintains the tension of the lace. Similarly, threads travelling from left to right have one continuous thread to be found on the extreme right at the completion of each stitch. Ground that appears uneven invariably has inaccurate twists. In England it is usual to work the footside on the right hand side; on the continent it is worked on the left. For insertion it is worked on both sides. To work the footside there are two methods in common use; each achieves the same result, but the moment at which the catch pin and foot pin are put up is different.

### Method 1

has been described on page 12.

### Method 2

is the traditional way and used by many experienced lacemakers today.

*Footside.* Take the fourth pair from the edge – this has three twists on already – and work two cloth stitches towards the edge through the two passive pairs.

Twist the weaver three times.

Put up the foot pin to the left of the weaver between the last pairs worked.

Work a cloth stitch with the two outside pairs and twist each pair three times.

Ignore the outer pair and cloth stitch back through the two passive pairs.

Twist the weaver three times.

*Catch pin and stitch.* Put up the catch pin to the right of the weaver, between the last worked pairs.

Work a ground stitch with the weaver and the pair to the left of it. (The stitch is worked to the side of the pin already in position.)

*Ground.* Use the left of these pairs and the next to the left to work a ground stitch. The pin is put up between the pairs.

To maintain a straight footside the pins should be left in the lace for the length of the pricking. Photograph 100, pricking 101 and diagram 102 show a pattern with the normal footside and ground. The ground runs directly into cloth diamonds which in turn provides pairs for the honeycomb.

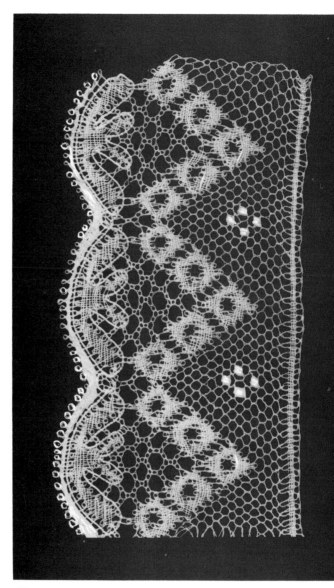

100

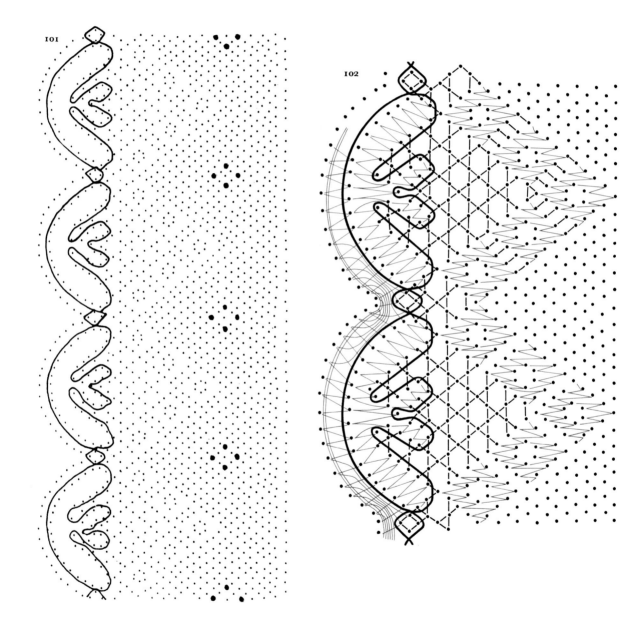

## TO PLOT THE HOLES FOR CUCUMBER FOOT ON A GROUND PRICKING

(Refer to diagram 103.) The usual footside arrangement is shown at A. At B the holes have been repositioned to work cucumber foot. Note that the space allowed for the tally is the same as for any other row of ground, but that the two rows of holes inside the footside are exactly level with each other. To add this foot to any edging, prick the pattern completely except for the footside. Take a piece of clear film, place it under the original pricking and transfer the catch pin and footside rows of holes onto the film. Place the film over the new pricking until the two rows of holes are in the correct position and complete the pricking.

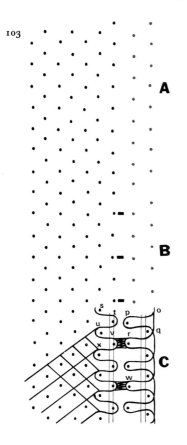

## TO WORK CUCUMBER FOOT

(Refer to diagram 103 and C.) The outer row of holes retains its function as footside, but the catch pin stitch is moved. The footside pin at o is worked and the inner pair travels as usual through the two passive pairs in cloth stitch. The pin is put up at p, the weaver is twisted three times and the pair returns to the footside to pin q. Again the inner pair from q travels back with two cloth stitches, the weaver is twisted three times and the pin put up at r. Ignore all four edge pairs as they remain on the edge throughout. Hang one pair on a pin at s and work cloth stitch through two pairs to the right. These pairs become the inner passive pairs and remain in this position. Put up pin t to the left of the weaver and twist the weaver three times. Work back to the left through the two new passive pairs in cloth stitch and twist the weaver three times. Use the weaver and the next pair to the left to make a ground stitch; put up the *catch* pin u to the right of both pairs. Of these pairs the left hand pair continues to work the row of ground, but the right hand pair works two cloth stitches to the right. It is twisted three times and pin v is put up to the left of it. Pairs from v and r work a tally. If the tally weaver came from the right hand side pair it will complete the tally on the left hand side. The footside edge can be worked to the next tally at w. The pair from the tally at v works to the left through the passive pairs to catch pin at x.

The outer rows of holes (i.e. from o and p) are used for a cloth tape with a footside edge on one side. It is linked to the rest of the lace by tallies which are usually made at alternate holes. The row of holes from t are in the position of the footside in a normal footside. However, in cucumber foot the row serves to support the edge pair with twists but does not become a straight edge. The row of holes from s is the catch pin row.

104(a)    104(b)

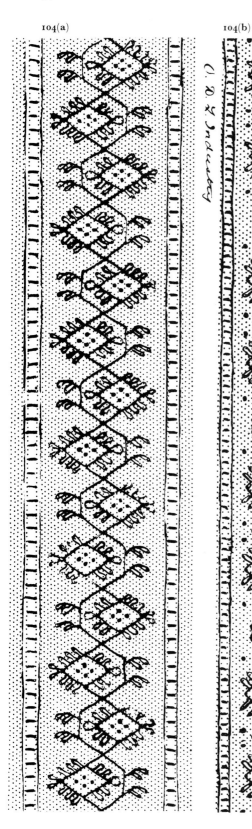

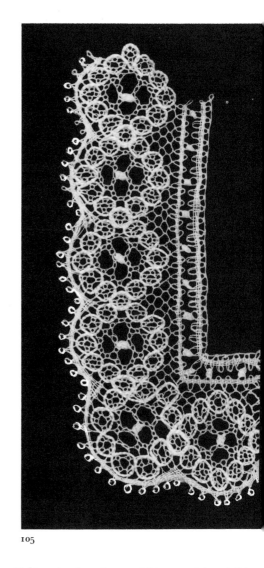

105

The old Downton insertions, prickings 104(a) and (b), show interesting forms of this type of decoration. Notice the closeness of the holes and consequently the fineness of thread required. Pricking 104(a) has both rows of passive threads within the ground, therefore catch pins will be required on both sides of both trails. Pricking 104(b) has the usual arrangement of holes. The prickings are based on a grid at 57° and there are 20 holes to one inch (25mm).

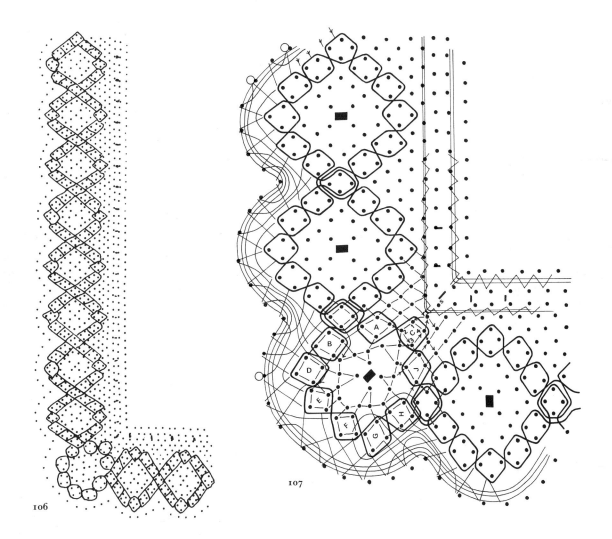

106

107

For practice refer to photograph 105, pricking 106 and diagram 107. The buds in the corner are worked in letter order. Where necessary the pin holes within a bud are numbered to indicate working order. A tally is worked diagonally across the corner; this is essential to hold the corner footside in position. It is preferable to work the tally the first time that pin s is used. The second time, the pair is twisted and passed round the pin. Pin t is used twice – before the pair enters C at 1 and after C is completed at 4.

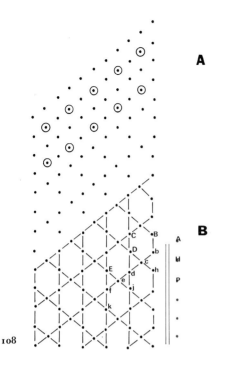

**A**

**B**

108

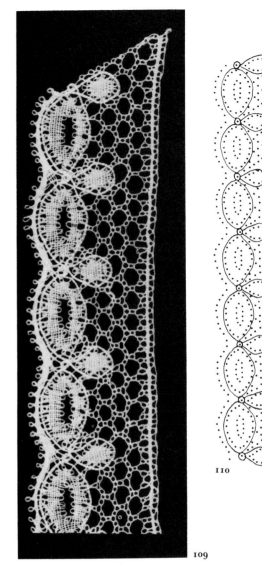

109

110

## HONEYCOMB

This is used as a ground occasionally but is more often to be found as a filling, and is without doubt the most important stitch after point ground in the working of Bucks Point lace. The grid is made from the point ground grid (refer to diagram 108) and note that certain holes are omitted, 108(a) shows the making of the grid and 108(b) the method of working. In order to work the fillings in the irregular old patterns it is necessary to understand fully the directions in which the threads travel. Pairs travel diagonally both ways as in point ground but some pairs fall vertically. The gap row pin holes are always on a vertical line. Many lace-makers think of working honeycomb with 'continuous' and 'gap rows. In the past the stitch was called 'five pin', the five pins being the X, and the centre pin was the gap row pin. This emphasised the correct use of pairs for the gap row and consequently for the continuous row below it. Another way of looking at honeycomb is to find the diamond shapes. The first pin to be worked in any diamond must be at the point of the obtuse angle. Variations of honeycomb provide a collection of interesting fillings; these appear in patterns throughout the book. (Refer to diagram 238 on page 154.)

### To plot honeycomb ground and footside
(Refer to diagram 108.) 108(a) shows the arrangement of holes; the footside is added in the same way as in the point ground pricking.

### To work honeycomb ground and footside
(Refer to diagram 108.) 108(b) is used to explain the method. Hang two pairs on the footside pin at A, twist three times and cover the pin with cloth stitch and three twists. Ignore the outer pair and take the inner pair through two passive pairs hung in order on B. Twist twice and make a honeycomb stitch with the pair hanging from C. Put up pin at b and cover with honeycomb stitch. Hang two pairs in order on D and E. With the left hand pair from b continue to work the continuous row d, e and so on. To work the footside at H, take the fourth pair from the edge (i.e. the pair from b) and work the normal Bucks footside. On return from the footside pin H the weaver passes through the two passive pairs and receives two twists before working the honeycomb stitch, pin h, honeycomb stitch with the pair from c. The gap row is worked j, k, and so on. To work footside pin P take the fourth pair from the

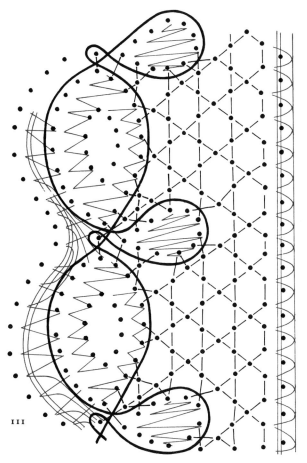

111

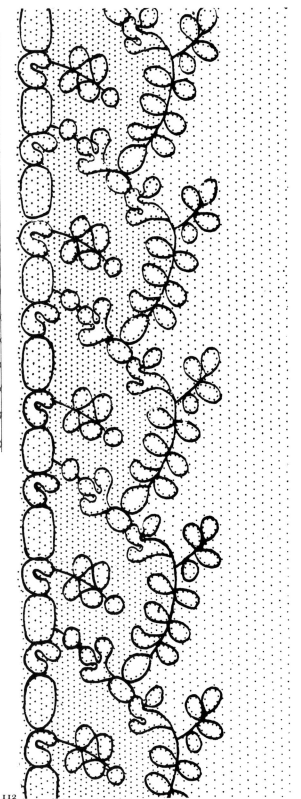

112

edge and work in the usual manner. The most common
error that occurs in honeycomb ground is to forget the
footside pin before working the gap row. For added interest
a honeycomb ground can be given to some narrow
edgings. However, to keep the pattern regular and easy to
work there should be an even number of diagonal rows to
one pattern repeat, to accommodate the 'gap' and the
'continuous' rows.

It is important to select a pattern without **too** much
honeycomb on the headside. (Refer to photograph 109,
pricking 110 and diagram 111.) In the illustration in the
North Bucks Lace Association catalogue this pattern,
known as the Bow, has point ground. However, as the
pattern is narrow and the design is worked in cloth stitch, it
lends itself very well to the honeycomb ground. There are
eight diagonal working rows to each pattern repeat and it
can be pricked with the honeycomb ground as shown. It is
important to maintain the vertical and diagonal lines in
the ground to achieve good tension; this is difficult when
they enter the solid cloth shape. From the diagram it will
be seen that in three positions the threads work honeycomb
stitches without pins. The lace can be worked with
reference to the diagram. Note that the gimp thread works
a figure of eight movement. Another pattern using the
honeycomb ground is shown on page 132.

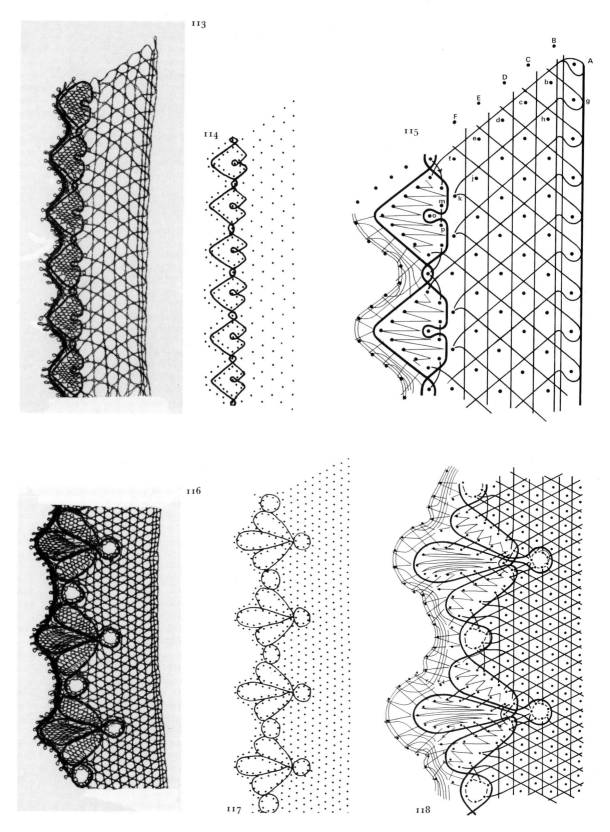

## KAT STITCH

Pricking 112 is an old kat stitch pattern. The lace is usually very wide and worked in black thread. When working it is essential to maintain the vertical and diagonal lines in the ground. Any discrepancy results in a poor and untidy piece of work; it is better to add extra pairs to maintain these lines, or to cross pairs before use as described for the honeycomb pattern on page 77. Photograph 113 illustrates kat stitch with the holes placed very far apart; this facilitates the understanding of the stitch but is not very attractive. (Refer to the pricking 114 and diagram 115.)

### To begin kat stitch ground

Hang three pairs of bobbins round pin A. Twist the right hand two threads three times and work cloth stitch and twist with these from right to left through the other two pairs on pin A. Hang two pairs in order on pins B to F inclusive. Take the left hand pair from A and work cloth stitch and twist through the two pairs on B. Put up pin b between the pairs of the last stitch worked (i.e. to the right of the pair travelling from A). Take this pair and work cloth stitch and twist through the two pairs hanging on C. Put up pin c between the pairs of the last stitch worked (i.e. to the right of the travelling pair). Continue to work in cloth stitch and twist, working two stitches and putting a pin up between the pairs of the second stitch.

Note that one pair moves from the footside to the head and this gives the straight line and good tension.

There are two pairs hanging between each pin; the pins are not covered. Take the two pairs hanging between e and f and work a cloth stitch and twist; no pins are put in. Take the pairs between d and e and work a cloth stitch and twist; no pin is put in. Continue towards the footside until the two pairs to the right of b have been worked together and there are pairs left on the footside.

### To work kat stitch ground

There are two passive twisted pairs on the footside as well as the outside pair. Begin by taking the third pair from the outside edge, work cloth stitch and twist through the two pairs to the edge. Put up pin g inside two pairs, twist the outer pair twice more and leave it to the side of the pillow. Use the other pair to cover pin g with cloth stitch and twist. Take the pair which completed this sequence (i.e. the third from the right) and work cloth stitch and twist through the next two pairs. Pin h is put up between the last pairs. Continue to j. It will soon become obvious that the pins support the diagonals where they cross and that the first of

the two stitches takes the diagonal through a passive vertical pair. To achieve the linking of ground to pattern a clear understanding of this is essential. The second row of ground is worked without pins. The stitch worked between the pins makes the diagonal (travelling to the right) cross through a vertical pair.

### To link ground and pattern

The single honeycomb pin between the hearts is enclosed with gimp threads. The right hand pair from this pin works cloth stitch and twist with the diagonal pair in order that the diagonal can enter the heart continuing a straight line. The heart weaver passes out round the gimp to the ground. The diagonal pair must be taken through the vertical pair before it works cloth and twist before and after pin k. It travels back through the vertical pair before it can be used in the next diagonal row of ground. Pin o is a nook pin; one pair is left hanging from m. In this pattern the pair from m is not required in the ground and re-enters the heart directly at p. Note that the pair from the right hand side of the bottom heart pin has to cross the previous pair in order to maintain the diagonal line.

### A typical black silk pattern

(Refer to photograph 116, pricking 117 and diagram 118.) The lace may be worked in a variety of ways; the design is sometimes filled with half stitch as shown in the photograph, but it is also worked as open holes surrounded by honeycomb stitches. The number and arrangement of holes varies from one pattern repeat to the next. Normally the lacemaker deals with each situation as it arises, for the aim is to achieve a pleasant result and not an exact copy which, when subjected to a geometric grid, may become angular and less attractive. Extra stitches are worked as required in order to maintain the vertical and diagonal lines. As far as possible one vertical pair should be retained close to the pattern feature as this fills the space and gives continuity. Unwanted pairs may accumulate temporarily and these may be carried with the gimp. (The blue lines on the right hand side of the honeycomb rings indicate spare pairs carried in this manner until required again.) The working diagram suggests one way of using the pairs to work the pattern. However, it must be remembered that the more complicated patterns may be worked successfully in a variety of ways at the discretion of the worker. More complex kat stitch patterns with prickings are on pages 127 and 128.

# 6 The inaccurate pattern –
## *How to Improve the Pricking*

Considerable time and care are required to produce an accurate pricking. Today most prickings are made from photocopies or from printed prickings in books. Occasionally the old drafts are used, or copies of the old drafts, and sometimes lacemakers will take a copy from a well-used pricking. One of the easiest ways to get a good pricking is to prick through the holes of another pattern, provided that the original is accurate

## GENERAL POINTS CONCERNING THE PRICKING OF BUCKS POINT PATTERNS

1. Use a Sharp 8 sewing needle in a pin vice or pricker; anything thicker will damage the original pricking and make holes that are too large to keep the pins firm when making the lace.

2. Always make the pricking onto vellum or the tough, glazed brown card that is readily available from the lace equipment stockists.

3. Prick the footside separately from the rest of the pattern. Place two pins, one in a hole at either end of the footside, so that a ruler can be pushed against them. Prick in the footside holes along the edge of the ruler to achieve a straight line.

4. Always prick the ground and fillings along the diagonal working line; use a ruler to ensure that the lines are straight.

5. The pattern should be fastened to the card using drawing pins. As these make large holes and have large heads to keep the pieces firmly together, the complete work may be lifted from the pricking board so that the lacemaker is able to examine the underside of the pricking and note any holes that may have been missed.

6. If drawing pins are used there is another advantage when pricking elaborate patterns. It is possible to prick the main features first, remove the master copy, mark in the gimp lines, put the master back in position and then prick the ground and fillings. This results in a better gimp line and saves considerable time.

7. Always make at least one paper copy; place the paper between the master copy and the card for the best results. This copy is used for reference when making the lace; for example, the working of honeycomb may be marked in to indicate how pairs will be required from pattern features.

## TO MAKE A PRICKING FROM A MASTER PRICKING

This is straightforward: place the master over a paper and the card and pin everything firmly to a pricking board. The pricking is made according to the recommendations given above. However, if any hole appears to be out of position it should not be pricked. Eventually it can be added 'by eye' on the new pricking. Never correct the original; double pricking is confusing and difficult to use.

## TO MAKE A PRICKING FROM A PHOTOCOPIED LENGTH

(Refer to diagram 119.) At first sight this appears to be a very easy way to obtain a pricking quickly; however, the result is often disappointing as it is difficult to work in straight lines and prick through the centre of each dot. Using a pencil with a sharp point, draw in vertical lines as shown in the diagram in blue. When pricking the footside holes, use the dots as a general guide but prick the holes along the straight line of the ruler. Similarly, when pricking the ground, prick along the working diagonal using a ruler and make the holes where the ruler crosses the vertical pencil lines.

## TO MAKE A PRICKING FROM A DRAFT

The old vellum drafts are usually very accurate, but if a photocopy is used refer to pages 91 and 92; it is necessary to make an accurate copy as described above. Many of the old drafts are exactly one repeat of a pattern; it is usual to find two or three holes marked with ink rings and this indicates that these are the only holes that overlap the next repeat. They are used to get the repeat in the correct position.

To prepare the pricking place a sheet of cartridge paper that is 50mm (2in) longer and 50mm (2in) wider than required onto a pricking board. Place six pieces of paper under the draft at the top of the long piece of paper and pin them together with drawing pins. Prick the complete pattern repeat. Lift all paper to check that every hole has been pricked, separate the papers and mark the gimp lines on all copies. Draw in the footside position on the long sheet of paper. Using a ruler and a pricker scratch a line horizontally across each repeat pricking just above the top row of holes. Fold each pattern repeat on the scored line. Place

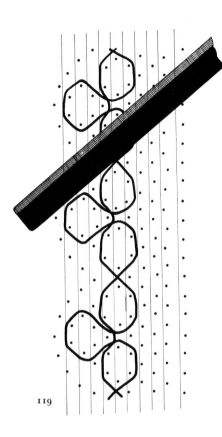

119

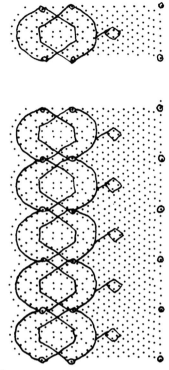

120

one repeat in the correct position on the long sheet; fasten by putting pins in the repeat holes only. Ascertain that the footside is straight and in line with the undercopy. Similarly, place the other repeats in position and fasten them together with adhesive tape well away from the pin holes, to keep the pieces in position for pricking. The procedure described for the photocopied length should be adopted to ensure accuracy. Pricking 120 is made using a draft; a photograph of the lace appears on page 139. Occasionally prickings are in two pieces and in these cases an overlap has been allowed. (See, for example, pricking 165.) The lacemaker will join the pieces so as to achieve pattern continuity.

## TO IMPROVE A POOR COPY OF AN ELABORATE PATTERN

It is essential to understand the pattern and have a clear idea of the working method. Most old patterns are extremely fine with the holes very close together, and they frequently appear inaccurate through continual use. Pricking 121 is a North Bucks Lace Association pattern and is in very good order; however, it will be used to illustrate the points discussed here. Before repricking any pattern try to establish the following:

1. Is the ground a kat stitch or a point ground?
2. If ground is used as a filling, it is pricked at the same angle and the same size as the ground at the footside?

3. Is the honeycomb filling made from the same grid as the ground?
4. Are the ground and the fillings at the same angle? The pattern on page 70 has a finer grid and steeper working line for the honeycomb.
5. How are the less usual fillings worked?
6. Is the picot arrangement satisfactory? Some old patterns have the picot holes very close together and today the pins are not fine enough to get good results. Sometimes these holes may be repricked farther apart. Is the picot line regular or should the holes be repricked more evenly?
7. Which parts of the pattern cannot be worked successfully and therefore must receive attention?
8. Is the footside straight?

The lacemaker has to decide if the pricking in its present state can be used to produce a good piece of lace and, if not, whether it is possible to make some adjustments. Slight irregularities in the ground will not affect the result as the tension depends on the correct number of twists and a taut thread. Poor fillings can be omitted and added later, as explained below. Misshapen pattern features or an uneven picot line can be altered if pricking from a paper copy. It is easier to make an exact copy from a pricking, as the pricker has definite holes to use. However, if the edges or shapes require adjustment it is essential to work on a paper copy. Refer to pricking 122, which has no obvious footside, and to the accompanying photograph 123. The lace should be appliquéd onto net or fabric; it is usual for the deeply

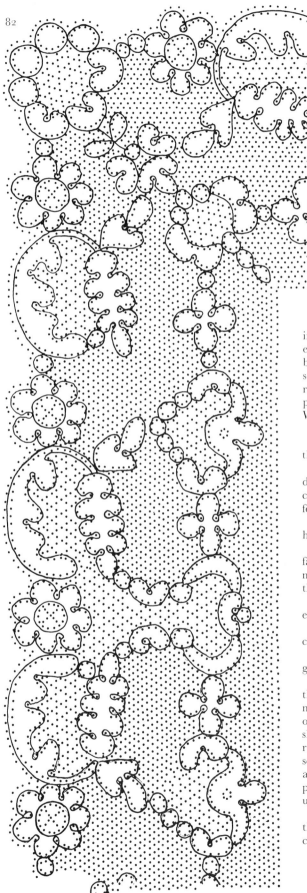

121

indented edge to be sewn to the fabric and the straighter edge to be decorated with picots. The complete length can be made accurate, or one pattern repeat may be used several times. Difficulty may be experienced putting the repeats together as old patterns may have many misplaced pinholes. A method to overcome this problem is shown. Work as follows:

1. Select a good area of pattern.

2. Draw horizontal lines across the pricking to indicate the extent of one repeat.

3. Draw in the vertical lines for the ground; add the diagonal working lines. This may seem tedious but it does clarify the use of holes in small areas between pattern features.

4. Draw in the vertical and diagonal lines to indicate the honeycomb.

5. Place two pieces of paper under the master copy and fasten all three together very firmly. Adjust the holes as necessary prick in the pattern features. Add the picots and the footside edge.

6. Prick two holes, well away from the pattern area, at either end of the repeat lines.

7. Separate the papers, mark in the gimp lines on both copies.

8. Draw in the repeat lines using the pin holes as a guide.

9. Scratch a line, using a pricker and a ruler, just above the top repeat line on one copy. Fold along the line and match the patterns. There should be one picot hole and one footside hole common to both papers. Similarly, there should be holes, in the pattern features that fall on the repeat line, that are common to both. As the pattern is old some adjustment may be necessary. It is important to adjust *one* side of the repeat line only, i.e. alter one piece of paper but not both. When the result is satisfactory, the untouched copy is discarded and the altered copy is used.

10. Place the master over this adjusted copy and fix in the correct position using the same holes at the four corners. Prick in the ground and the honeycomb but do

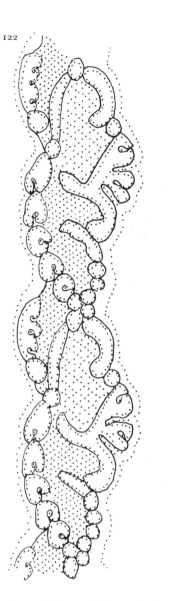

122

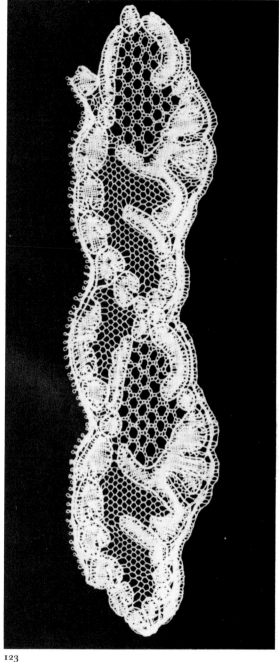

123

not attempt to place a filling at either end as it will not match when the repeats are put together.

11. Make several copies of this pattern. Mark in the gimp lines. Indicate the repeat lines and score the top of each as previously described. Fold the top of each back and match them to make the length.

12. This length of pattern is pricked onto card ready for use. All gimp lines are added.

13. Choose ground of similar size and angle to that in the pattern, and prick onto clear rigid plastic. Always place the plastic under the grid or pricking and prick through to get an accurate copy. Immediately mark in the position of the footside and direction of working. Place this over the pattern and prick in the required ground holes. By using this method there can be no difficulty where repeats are joined. The method is similar to that described when preparing a pricking from lace (see page 96).

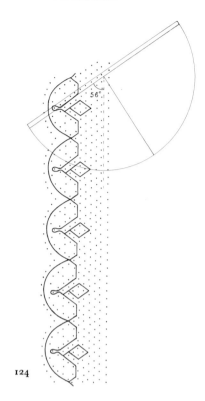

124

## TO MAKE A PRICKING USING A GRID

It is necessary to ascertain the angle between the footside and the diagonal working line on the original pricking. (Refer to illustration 124.) As it is easier to read the angle along the footside edge, the base line of the protractor is set along the working diagonal. Select a suitable grid; methods of preparing and collecting grids were discussed in Chapter 5. Refer to pricking 125. It is worked at 52°. Refer to illustration 126(a) and mark the line of the gimp onto the grid.

(Refer to illustration 126(b).) Ring the holes that are not required for the honeycomb. Note that there is one extra hole to be ringed so that the gimp can travel into the honeycomb easily. Holes to be omitted in the fingers in ground are ringed also.

(Refer to illustration 126(c).) Place the grid over strong paper and prick in the honeycomb. With the exception of the outside footside row prick in the ground. Add the footside (if necessary, refer to page 69). Draw in the gimp lines. Use a ruler to mark in one pattern repeat as shown in the illustration in blue. The horizontal lines are drawn through the actual holes and both lines must fall across the same holes just one pattern repeat apart.

Draw in the curve for the picots. Measure the distance from the footside on the repeat lines as the holes must fall in the same position. There are 17 picots on the original pricking; prick in the holes on the repeat lines and one in the centre of the curve. Draw lines to cut the curved line to indicate picot positions; these lines can be erased more easily than dots should it be necessary to adjust the first attempt.

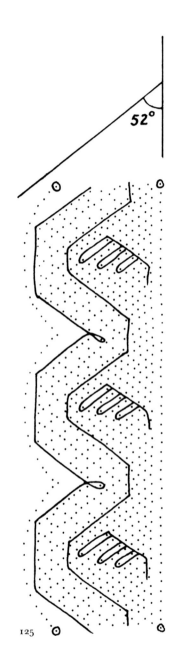

125

(Refer to illustration 126(d).) Prick in the remaining picot holes. The master pricking is complete. It is possible to plan a length of pricking on a grid, or one repeat may be used as described previously. To reprick to obtain a number of repeats it is essential to add the ringed holes which assist when matching repeats. Every hole along the top repeat line will be pricked. Only three holes on the lower repeat line should be pricked. The others will be omitted. Illustration 126(d) shows the holes ringed in blue to facilitate the

126(a)

126(b)

126(c)

126(d)

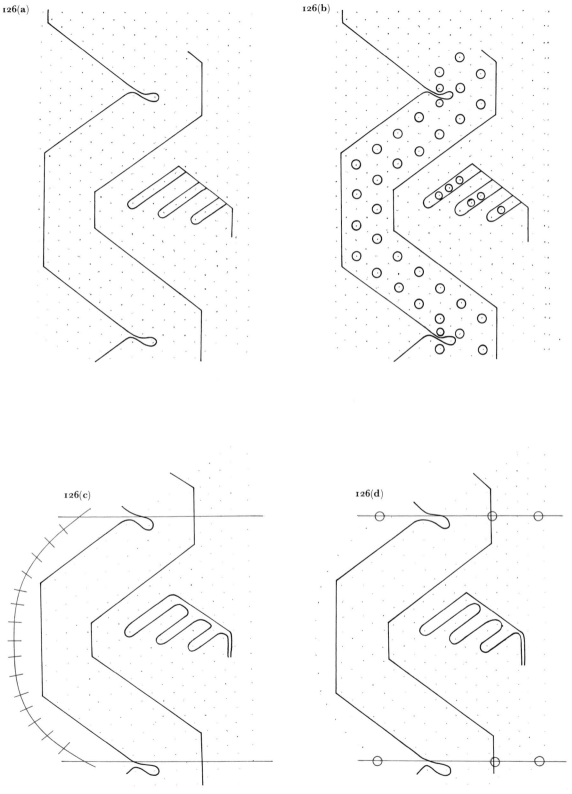

preparation of the length. Photograph 127 and diagram
128 give guidance on the making of the lace. More elaborate
patterns present considerable difficulty when remaking the
pricking, and normally the lacemaker should adjust the
pattern features and reprick the fillings as described on page
83. It is unwise to use a grid and start from the beginning as
the original beauty can rarely be recaptured. However, the
lacemaker interested in this will find helpful advice on page
95 where the making of lace patterns from pieces of lace or
photographs is discussed.

The lace in photograph 129 has been made from
pricking 130(b) which is a slight modification of 130(a).

127

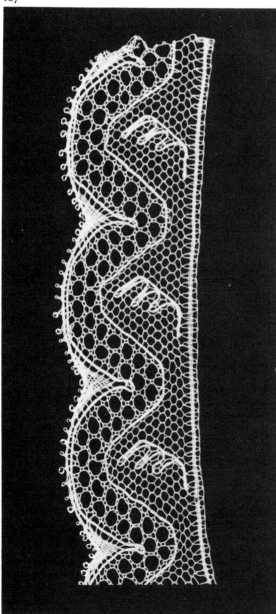

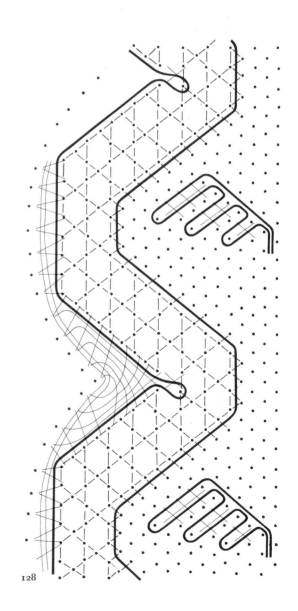

128

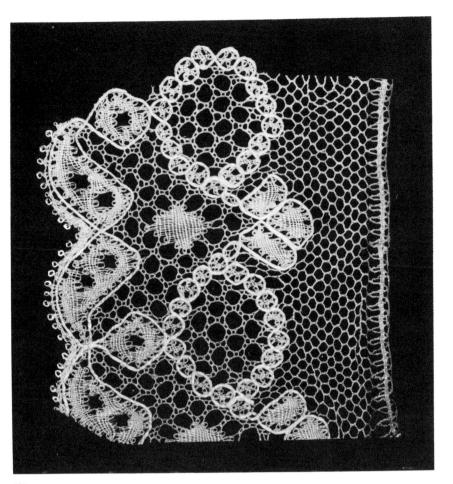

129

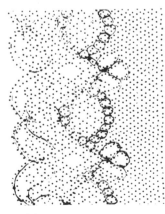

130(a)

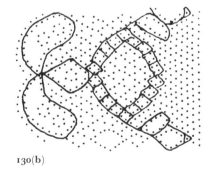

130(b)

# 7 Pattern Drafts

The pattern draft is the master copy from which the prickings were made. Luton Museum and Art Gallery has a large collection and these are invaluable to the twentieth-century lacemaker. It is an excellent plan to work the lace from a draft copy, as there is usually a range of possible interpretations. Illustration 131 shows 12 small pieces of lace and the draft patterns accompany them. Illustration 132 shows 20 drafts; the Museum and Art Gallery generously allow lacemakers to have photocopies. In addition the photographed sheets of the Lace Dealer's sample book are available as single sheets. These are useful to the student who wishes to study old lace to facilitate the making of the elaborate patterns. Methods of making prickings from lace or photographs of lace are discussed in the next chapter.

131

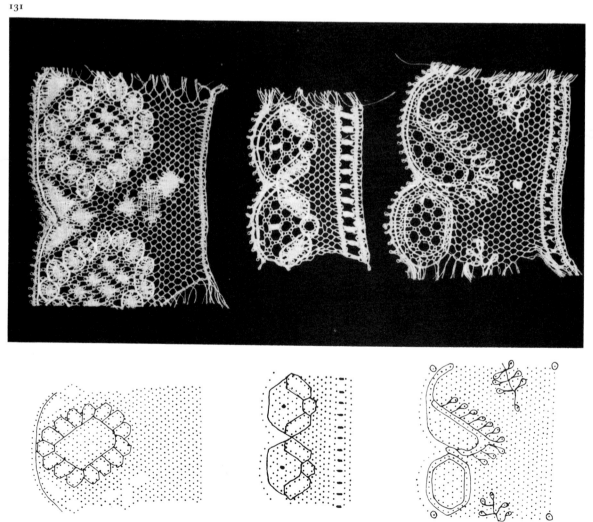

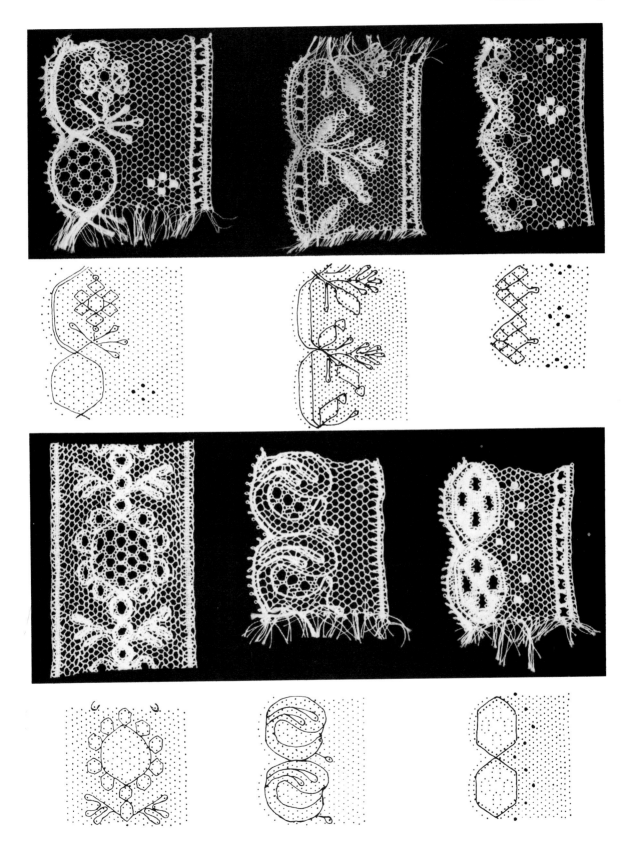

No 175

No 175

No 175

Agent 4

Agent 4

3

Vincent

for Black

for Black

132

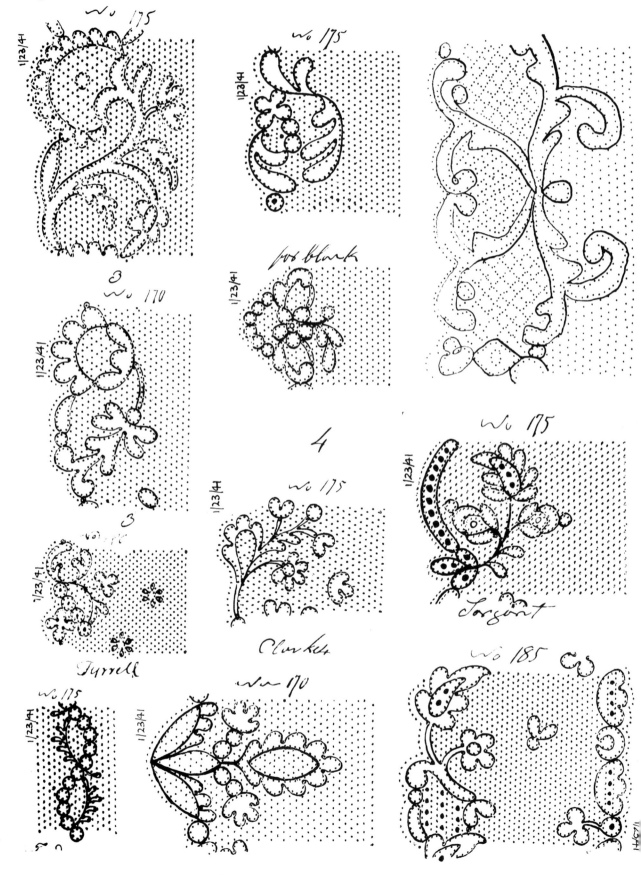

# 8 Making Prickings from Lace

Prickings for the simple geometric designs can be made easily, but the wider, more elaborate patterns present many problems. The angle between footside and working line must be ascertained as this controls the design. (Refer to Chapter 5.) The lace must lie flat with the footside straight. If necessary it should be dampened and pinned out so that it can be studied more easily. Refer to photograph 133 and work as follows:

1. Using a protractor, find the angle between the footside and the line of working. Refer to diagram 124 on page 84; it is easier to read the angle along the footside edge. The ground in the horseshoe pattern has been worked at 60°.

2. Count the number of holes to each inch along the footside; in this pattern there are 12.

3. Select a grid at 60° with approximately 12 holes to one inch. If a finer lace is required a grid with holes closer together may be used but the 60° angle *must* be retained.

4. To facilitate the planning of the pricking it is considered easier to work on a large scale and work on the fine grid later. Large scale grids are given on pages 162 and 164.

5. (Refer to illustration 134(a).) Count rows of ground to find the position of the gimp thread and draw straight lines to enclose the honeycomb area. The headside curve will appear distorted but this will be remedied later. Mark in two pattern repeats so that the passage of threads between repeats can be checked.

6. With a sharp pointed pencil mark in the position of the footside holes.

7. (Refer to illustration 134(b).) Place two papers under the grid and prick the ground and footside only.

8. In the honeycomb area ring the holes that will not be required. Remove one piece of paper and prick the honeycomb as shown on the second repeat.

9. The grid is no longer required and can be kept for future use.

10. Count the holes on the honeycomb edge and ring those which are not required. Refer to the illustration and draw in a curved line as indicated in blue. The six holes on either side of centre should be repositioned on the curved line.

11. (Refer to illustration (134(c).) Reposition the piece of paper with ground and footside exactly underneath and prick the adjusted honeycomb shape onto this paper. The top copy can be discarded; the bottom copy is correct.

12. (Refer to illustration 134(d).) Count the number of picots on the lace. There are 11 including the picots that fall on the repeat line. Draw a curved line, but leave sufficient space to accommodate the passive pairs between gimp and picots. Remember that there will be two pairs at the top of the curve but more will accumulate between repeats. Mark the centre picot, and the point where the curves meet. Add four on either side, and space them evenly. Put clear plastic under the pricking and prick the picots for one repeat onto the pricking and the plastic, which will be used to position the picots on the other repeat.

13. Draw horizontal lines to indicate two pattern repeats; on the lower line, ring three holes which will be used to set the repeats in line to make the length.

14. The pattern can be drawn out and pricked over one grid, but the grid cannot be used again. By using several pieces of paper, which may sound complicated when explained here, the grid can be removed when the essential holes have been pricked, and further work and alteration can be drawn and pricked through one of the paper copies. The completed pricking, 135, is given alongside the working diagram, 136.

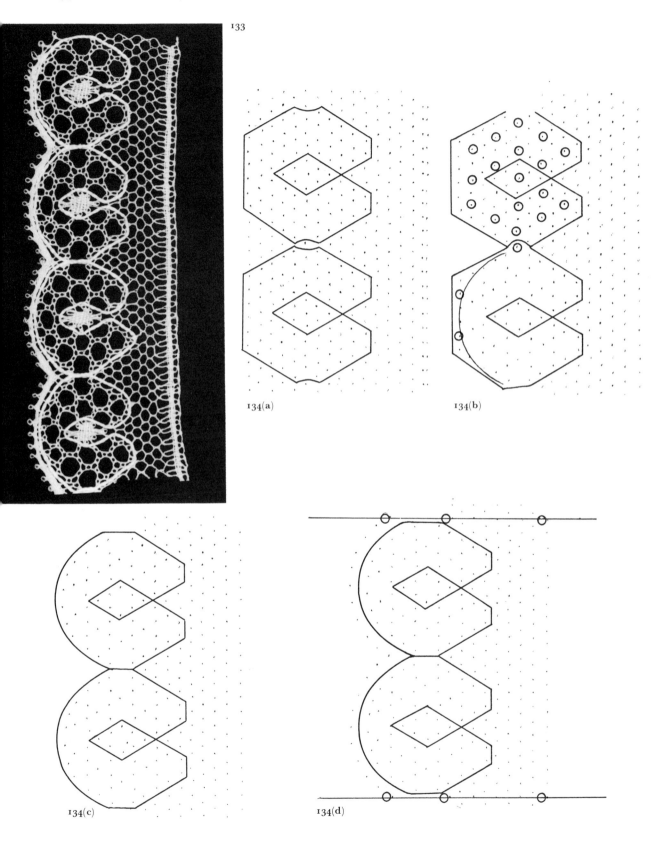

133

134(a)

134(b)

134(c)

134(d)

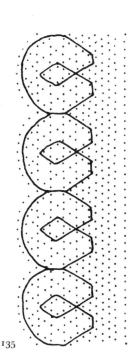

135

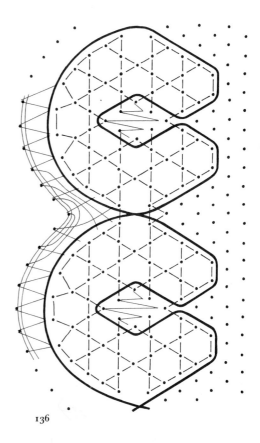

136

## ELABORATE PATTERNS

These are difficult to copy, and sometimes it is almost impossible to make a pricking. The horseshoe pattern is regular and it is possible to plot the pin holes on a grid; originally the pattern was made in this way. The old designs were drawn and grids used to build up the ground and fillings. The holes within the pattern features were added last, with two considerations: firstly to create interesting and well-shaped designs, and secondly to place the holes so that pairs from ground and fillings could be used to advantage as easily as possible. Obviously it is not easy to prepare a pricking from lace, but a method is suggested as follows:

1. (Refer to photograph 137.) As this is a narrow edging it may be possible to work out the pricking over a grid, but a suitable grid is essential to achieve the correct effect. However, the lace will be used to describe a method of copying elaborate patterns to make prickings. To attempt to reproduce every stitch as a pinhole in a complex design is not practical, and any difference in angle, however slight, will alter the shape of the design. It will be considerably easier to draw the design on cartridge paper and build up the pricking gradually. Either (a) place a piece of thin paper over the lace and rub gently with cobbler's wax or a soft pencil to make a copy of the design (this can be

transferred to cartridge paper) or (b) referring to illustration 138(a), scratch a grid onto clear plastic and place it over the lace. Make a similar grid on paper and copy the design. Mark in the approximate position of the repeat lines and the footside; this is shown in blue in illustration 138(b).

2. Prick a grid at the correct angle (refer to Chapter 5).

3. Use the grid over the pattern to work out the position of the footside pins (refer to illustration 138(c).) It is important to take advantage of the grid over the diamond, so that a ground row will run directly to the point of the diamond for easy working. In addition, the horizontal repeat lines must cross the pattern in the same position; either both are drawn through foot pins or both are drawn through catch pins. Some adjustment to the design or position of repeat lines will be necessary.

4. Prick in the ground and the footside.

5. Trace the bottom features of the design, i.e. the two rings and the half ring, and draw in exactly above the repeat. This will simplify the plotting of the honeycomb holes. Make a grid for honeycomb, place it over this area and prick in the honeycomb.

6. (Refer to illustration 138(d).) Add the holes for the cloth rings and the diamond; ignore the complete rings

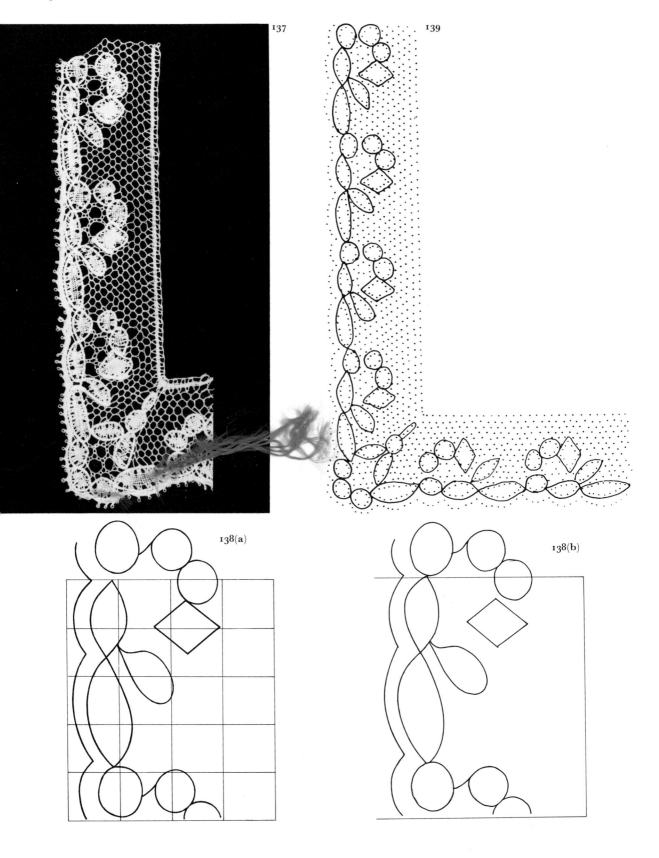

137

139

138(a)

138(b)

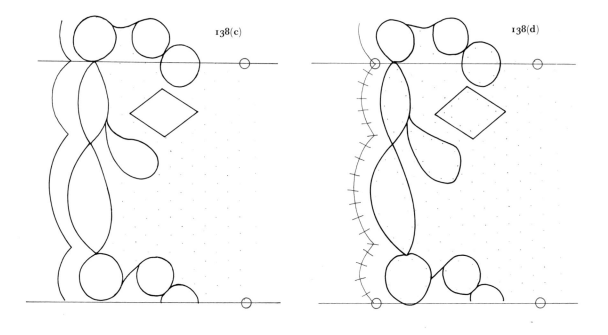

138(c)    138(d)

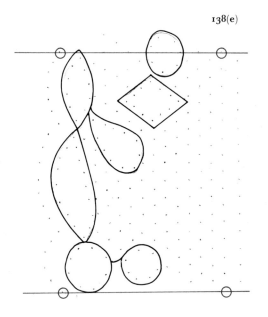

138(e)

above the repeat and the half ring at the bottom of the
repeat, as shown in the illustration. This requires thought
and skill, for the success of the pricking will depend on the
position of these holes. For example, it appears that only
three holes are necessary on either side of the diamond to
match the ground, and the pricking could be made in this
way. However, by referring to the lace it will be seen that
the stitches are much closer together in the cloth than in
the ground. It is common practice in old lace to carry extra
pairs in the cloth, and they travel from one cloth feature to
the next, or to work pins close together without necessarily
adding an extra pair at every pin. The beauty of old lace
depends upon the use of threads to achieve a pleasing
design that is married well with ground and filling.

7. Draw in the curves for the picot holes. Remember
that there are fewer picot holes than holes in the cloth
features at the edge, as the headside passives cross at the
inside of the curve and never leave a hole.

8. Illustration 138(e) shows the complete pricking for
one repeat. To maintain the pattern over the join certain
holes are pricked outside the repeat line, but they are
missed out at the other end of the repeat. Use the repeat as
described in Chapter 6. A complete pricking with corner is
shown in illustration 139. As it is possible to obtain a wide
variety of drafts or prickings, it is questionable whether or
not it is worth attempting to copy a piece of lace. The time
could be spent on a similar exercise, but instead of copying
from the past, an original design could be created.

# 9 Adaptation and Design

The ability to adapt or design depends on a knowledge of the basic principles of pattern construction and on the skill to make lace. An inexperienced lacemaker can design and work a simple hexagon, but more skill and understanding of old patterns is required to design and work a floral mat. At first, creating an original design may appear too complicated, but opportunity exists to alter and adapt old patterns. So many flounces, broad edgings and collars are unsuitable for modern use and it is unlikely that they will ever be worked again. Within the designs are many attractive features which can be used elsewhere. After achieving success with geometric designs and the adaptation of old patterns, enthusiasm will be aroused and many lacemakers will develop the confidence to create more original work.

Relevant to all adaptation and design is the need to know very clearly the purpose for which the lace is intended. For example, the exact size of a mount or frame must be ascertained, and the area within it that requires the lace must be indicated. Lace with a fine and intricate design over a large area will appear insignificant unless examined closely. A large design within a small frame requires careful consideration to obtain contrast and a light effect. The old mayflower filling on page 137 is very solid compared with the ordinary honeycomb on page 49. Although it is a very attractive old filling its use is limited to large areas. Cloth may be broken with holes (refer to pages 139 and 141) or twists can be given to passive pairs or to the weaver. The balance between cloth and the open areas of ground and fillings has to be studied carefully. Tallies add interest and 'break' a large expanse of ground, and gimp threads may be used for the same purpose. The size of the gimp thread needs consideration. It is both fascinating and worthwhile to study old lace to try to appreciate why particular fillings were chosen, and to imagine the effect of using alternative stitches. Almost any design can be worked using bobbins and thread, but consideration should be given to ease of working. It is necessary to make certain items quickly for sale whereas others made for interest may, after many hours working on design and lace, become family heirlooms.

The simplest way of making a design is to base it upon a grid. If the lacemaker understands how to make a pricking on a grid as described on pages 84 and 93 this will present no problems as the method is the same.

## TO MAKE HEXAGONAL MOTIFS

To make hexagonal motifs as shown in photograph 140 work as flollows:

1. Select a suitable grid according to the thread to be used. As each side of the motif as the same length, a 60° grid is necessary. Place it with the footside equivalent in a vertical position and mark clearly this and the diagonal working line. Through the centre draw a vertical line.

2. Outline the required shape; the top centre picot must fall on the vertical line. Pricking 141 accompanies the motifs in photograph 140. In motif (A) there is 18 holes on each side, and in motif (B), 20 holes. As these will be picot holes the position is indicated with a pencil line; they will be pricked later.

3. Prick holes on the next row all round to indicate the limit of the design.

4. Any features can be placed within this area provided that the grid is used. Motif (A) uses a cloth diamond as the focal point, and (B) uses a hexagon with tallies in honeycomb. The gimp and tallies in ground add weight to the design. Both motifs use small areas of cloth at the edge to add strength to the pattern. Every hole in these motifs, with the exception of the picots, can be pricked directly from the grid. When the pattern has been planned the holes should be pricked along diagonal lines to ensure accuracy.

5. The picots are set in position, slightly further from the rest of the holes, rather like a footside, in order to accommodate passive pairs. They should be pricked along a ruler to achieve a straight line.

### To work the hexagon

Work begins at the top picot pin and is finished at the bottom centre pin. Pairs are added on both sides and lace is made diagonally as usual; pairs will be thrown out along the bottom sides so that very few remain at the final pin hole. Diagram 142 indicates the method of working. Detailed diagram 143(a), (b) and (c) is labelled in the same way as the large diagram.

(Refer to diagram 143(a).) Make false picots as described on page 18 at A, B and C. Take the left hand pair from A through both pairs from B in cloth stitch. Take the right hand pair from A and work through both pairs from C in cloth stitch. These pairs become the outside passive pairs. Work the left hand pair from C and the right hand

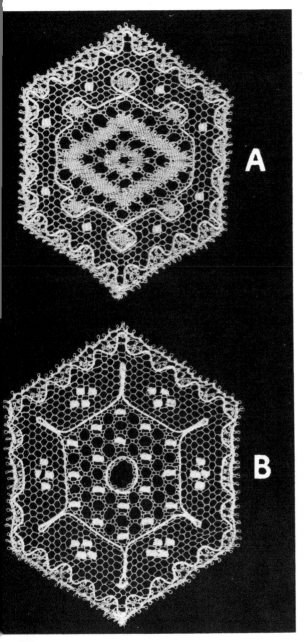

140

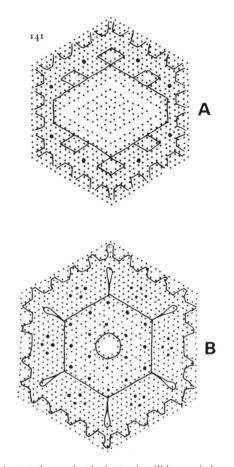

141

of picots to be made, the last pair will be carried as a third passive pair. Refer to diagram 143(c) and make picots on the other side, a false picot at J, and an ordinary picot at k; continue. These pairs will be used to work the cloth; there is no gimp between the passive pairs and the cloth. The hexagon should be worked completely except for the outside picot holes on the lower sides. To complete the use of the gimp thread, cross it and take it through the pairs from the ground pin, lay it back across the work and cut it off later.

To complete the picots and edge, take each pair out diagonally, work a picot and bring it back through two pairs as usual. As the passive pairs accumulate throw them back and discard them; there should be a maximum of three passive pairs at any time and therefore a total of six at the bottom. It is not easy to work the bottom centre pin. Work the three pairs on the left through the other three pairs in cloth stitch so that they lie flat. Take the outside pairs and cross them under the centre pairs, bring them to the top and tie them tightly together. Tie each pair of threads in the centre and then take the outside threads round the bundle once more and tie. Trim all threads to leave a tassel.

It is important to understand fully the method of designing and the way of working a hexagonal motif before working on a circular one.

pair from B together in cloth stitch to cross them; they become the inner passive pairs. The left hand pair from B works cloth stitch through one more pair to the right and the right hand pair from C works through one more pair to the left. A gimp thread is passed through these two pairs and enclosed with three twists. A ground stitch is made and pin T is put in position. There are two passive pairs on either side. Make a false picot at D and an ordinary picot at e. (Refer to diagram 143(b).) Repeat making false picots at F and H and ordinary picots at g and i. Continue until sufficient pairs are available. As there are an odd number

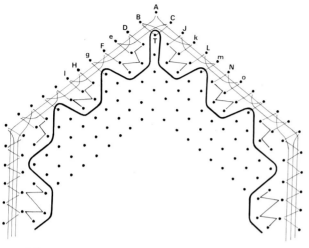

142

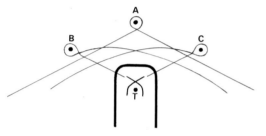

143(a)

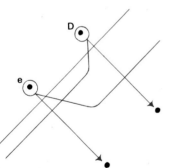

143(b)

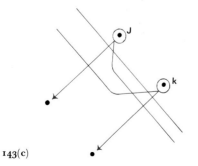

143(c)

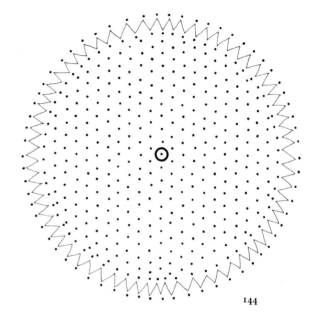

144

## TO PREPARE A CIRCULAR MOTIF

(Refer to diagram 144.) Take a grid and place several sheets of paper underneath. Use a pair of compasses to make a circle of the desired size. Indicate the position of the compass point on the paper copies. As the picot or footside holes will be sited on the line it is necessary to draw another line to indicate the extent of the ground. Adequate space should be allowed to accommodate the passive pairs. Using a straight edge, prick in every ground hole within the inner circle. If the grid is on paper and not required for future use, the holes on the inner circle line are pricked at both ends of every row of ground where the diagonal crosses the circle line. If the grid has to be removed, draw in the inner and outer circle and, using a straight edge, prick in the holes on the inner line. Always remove the grid before adding the outer picot or footside holes. Draw in a zigzag weaver line between the holes on the inner circle and outer line in order to set the position and number of holes required on the edge. This is shown in blue in the diagram. Prick the holes as evenly as possible; if a template of the correct size is available, the holes can be pricked against the side and a perfect circle achieved. Photograph 145 with pricking 146 shows motifs made by this method. The centre feature on pattern (A) was taken from a piece of lace plotted onto a grid and the simple feature in (B) was worked out directly onto the grid. All holes in pricking (B) are included so that the circular motif is available for a range of patterns.

### To work the picot edge

(Refer to pricking 146(a).) The outer ringed hole is the first to be worked; hang two pairs round a pin and make a false picot. Hang six pairs on a pin to one side of the work. Work the pairs from the false picot through the threads to one side of the pin in cloth stitch. The six pairs (i.e. six threads in each direction) lie across the work as passives

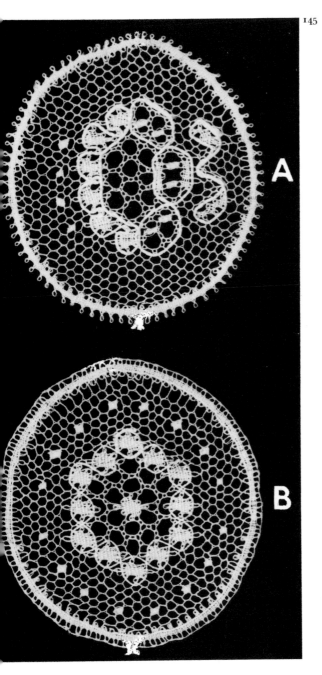

145

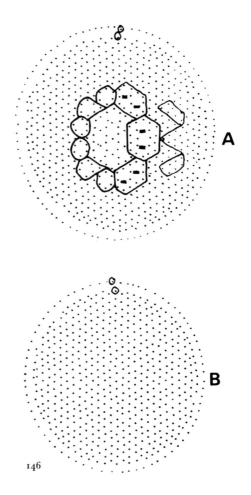

A

B

146

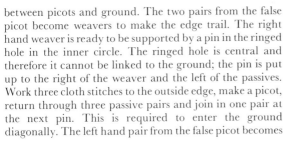

the weaver to work the left hand edge trail. Before it travels to the edge, a pair is added for the ground. The method of adding pairs is described on page 126. Pairs are added as required; if the ground is worked immediately pairs are available, the addition or removal of these will be understood. Pairs will be discarded into the edge trail when no longer required. When working the hexagon, pairs are joined in using false picots on the edge, but when working the circle the pairs are joined in on the *inner* edge of the trail. There is a definite weaver in the circle working the trail; in the hexagon, pairs travel through the passive pairs but a weaver exists only for a very short time at the widest part. When working the circle with a picot edge, three pairs of passives are recommended. This is not strictly correct for Bucks Point lace, but it does add strength as the outer pair has to travel an increased distance round the curve.

### To work the straight edge
(Refer to photograph 145(b) and pricking 146(b).) A pin is put in the ringed hole in the outer circle and four pairs are hung round the pin. The threads to the right of the pin are treated as two pairs and twisted three times each; cloth stitch and twist is worked with these pairs. The threads on

between picots and ground. The two pairs from the false picot become weavers to make the edge trail. The right hand weaver is ready to be supported by a pin in the ringed hole in the inner circle. The ringed hole is central and therefore it cannot be linked to the ground; the pin is put up to the right of the weaver and the left of the passives. Work three cloth stitches to the outside edge, make a picot, return through three passive pairs and join in one pair at the next pin. This is required to enter the ground diagonally. The left hand pair from the false picot becomes

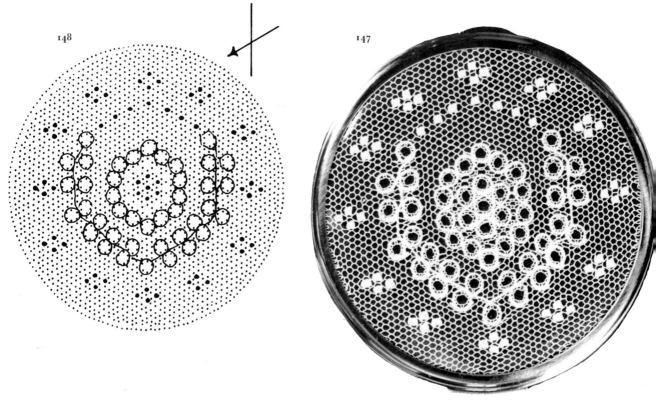

148

147

either side of the pin become weaver pairs, and the outer pairs wait temporarily as outer footside edge pairs. Hang four pairs, to become passive pairs, on a pin to one side. In turn work the weaver pairs with two cloth stitches through the threads on the right of the pin. These threads extend across the lace as passive pairs. The weaver threads hang inside ready to work pinholes in the inner row. They are used in the same way as in the pattern with the picot edge. It is not practical to introduce a catch pin when joining in threads on a curve. Nothing is added at the inner ringed hole and the weaver travels out to the right through two passive pairs, is twisted three times and works the footside pin. The other weaver joins in one pair and then travels out to the left through two passive pairs, is twisted three times and works the footside pin. In order to achieve a good edge, pairs are added on the inner edge of the passive pairs, and as with a normal footside the weavers are the same throughout.

It is not easy to get an even attractive result when putting the straight lines of ground against a curve. If there appears to be a large gap between the passive pairs and the ground stitches, introduce an extra row of ground pins and stitches. The pinholes may appear rather close to the curved edge but this will not be evident on the finished lace. In photograph 145(b) there are rather large holes at the top; the use of extra holes as described above would have avoided this. Extra rows of holes were added very close to the curve at the bottom of pricking 146(a); the photograph illustrates the improvement.

The lace mounted in a powder compact in photograph 147 is a geometric design worked out on a fine grid. It was planned with a plain footside edge, and mounted to avoid showing the edge. Edges can never be perfect unless a definite feature is introduced, and this is not always desirable as it may detract from the main pattern. Pricking 148 accompanies the photograph.

150 (a)

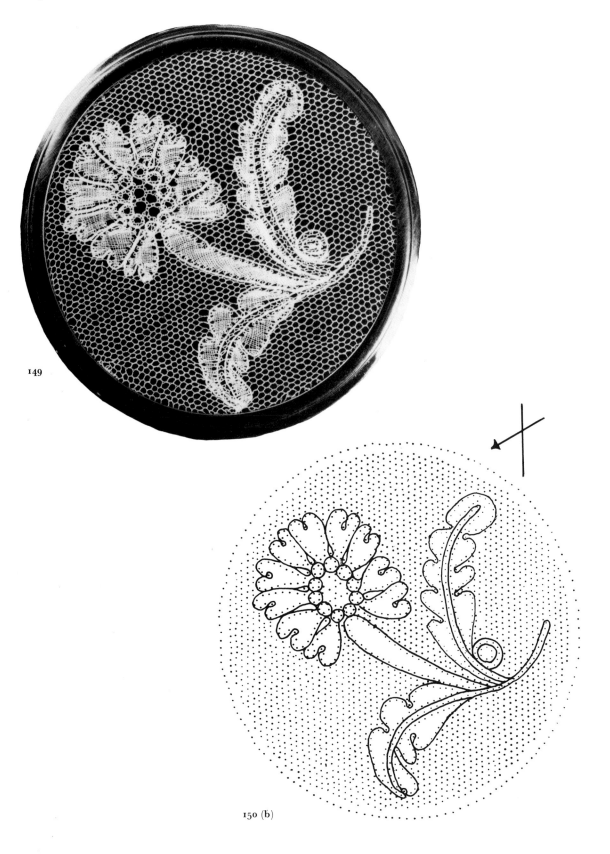

149

150 (b)

## MOTIFS MADE FROM OLD PATTERNS

The lace mounted in the powder bowl was a motif taken from an old North Bucks Lace Association pricking. Photograph 149 shows the mounted lace, pricking 150(a) is the original edging and pricking 150(b) the adaptation. The page from the N.B.L.A. catalogue illustrated on page 9 shows the 'Carnation' design. To make the motif, a circle was marked on the original pricking to include the carnation flower and both leaves. The centre point of the circle was noted, also the radius of the circle. Another circle was drawn inside to allow space for passive pairs. Several pieces of paper were fastened securely under the pricking and the centre of the circle was marked. Concentric circles were drawn onto the paper copies. The papers were fastened again and the motif and as much of the ground as possible pricked in. The actual pricking was removed and the work completed on a paper copy. First of all a piece of clear plastic was placed under the original pricking and an area of ground transferred. This was used to complete the ground on the copy. The holes on the concentric circle lines were added as described for previous patterns. It is important to indicate the footside equivalent and the diagonal working line in order to begin in the correct position.

## TO MAKE A SQUARE MOTIF

Occasionally it is desirable to make a square or rectangular motif. (Refer to photograph 151.) It is not possible to achieve a catch pin effect on all four sides, but the lace is neat and strong and suitable for insertion. Preparation of square pricking 152 and the interpretation of sketch 153 into a piece of lace are discussed below.

1. When using a design to make a pricking, it should be drawn out with definite lines onto thin card. The extent of the square should be indicated using a ruler.

2. Place several pieces of paper under the sketch and fasten them together firmly.

3. Place a transparent grid over the sketch, making certain that the footside equivalent is parallel to the side of the square. Mark this onto the card. Decide which lines of holes on either side are to be used for the catch pins and prick through the grid into the card and paper copies. Decide which holes will fall in a similar position at the top and the bottom, prick through grid and paper copies. These holes will be further apart than the true catch pin holes.

4. Prick all the ground holes that are within this boundary and outside the lines of the sketch.

5. Remove the grid. Prick the footside holes at either side. If necessary refer to Chapter 5.

6. Use a ruler to add a hole between every hole on the 'catch pin position' row at top and bottom. Prick the outer row of holes 'by eye'; these will be closer together than on the normal footside at the sides of the square. Diagram 154(a) shows the arrangement of holes.

7. Work on one piece of paper only; the others may be used for further attempts. Replace the grid and prick in as much of the design as possible using the grid holes. Remove the grid and complete the pricking. In order to prick the

design it is essential to understand the availability of pairs from the ground and where they will enter the pattern features. A knowledge of stitches and the ability to visualize the lace is needed for an interesting interpretation (refer back to photograph 151). Reasons for the choice of stitches are discussed below:

(a) The fruit would appear ugly and uninteresting in plain cloth stitch. As there are only three holes on each side there is insufficient space to include a centre hole. It would be difficult to make an attractive honeycomb arrangement unless the size and shape were altered. Vertical cloth emphasises the shape and tallies lighten the filling and add interest.

(b) The cornucopia requires an interesting filling and the texture must be very different from the ground. The area to be filled is small and narrow at one end, and a collection of isolated meaningless stitches at the narrow end must be avoided. A filling with a definite diagonal line which extends into this area will maintain the shape. Alternate honeycomb as described on page 145 is used. Six pin honeycomb rings are the obvious choice for the open end and, to add weight, tallies are placed in the rings.

(c) The leaf outline presents a problem as the area is small and the leaf pointed. There are a limited number of ways of working a hollow leaf, but as there are few pairs available the working of a solid leaf is not practical. The use of gimp is unusual and creates a different texture. The centre ring with leaves may seem foreign to Bucks Point lace, but it was occasionally used in old patterns. (Refer to photograph 236.)

(d) The space between the honeycomb rings and the leaves was left unfilled until the lace was on the pillow and the situation could be assessed with the pairs available. It was seen that pairs passing through each other in cloth filled the space and provided a neat background.

Everything except the leaves and the centre ring can be pricked through the grid. If necessary, the original grid may be used to make a grid for alternate honeycomb, but with experience the lacemaker may prick directly from the ground grid. It is necessary to work the design to discover any problems. In the case of this design it was found necessary to add honeycomb stitches around the curve of the cornucopia as the gimp did not remain in position.

### To work the square

(Refer to diagram 154(a).) Hang four pairs on pin A. The threads to the right of the pin are treated as two pairs and given three twists on each pair, and worked together with cloth stitch and three twists. The outside pairs become the footside edge pairs and the pairs either side of pin A work cloth stitch and twist to cover the pin. Hang two pairs on a pin at B. Allow the left hand pair from A to fall behind pin B and to the left of the pairs on B. The pair from A and the threads to the left of pin B are twisted three times and cloth stitch and three twists worked. Pin C is put up to the left of the right hand pair from A, two pairs are hung on C to fall to the left of the pair from A. The two threads to the right of pin C and the pair from A each receive three twists and are worked together with cloth stitch and three twists. The use

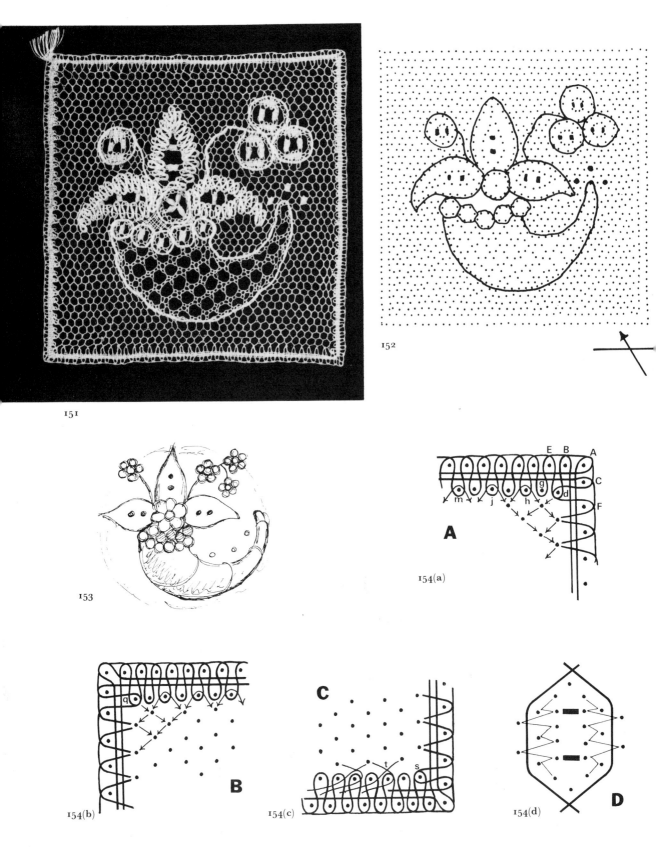

151

152

153

154(a)

A

154(b)

B

154(c)

C

154(d)

D

of the threads will be seen clearly in diagram 154(a). The left hand pair from C and the left hand pair from A become passive pairs across the top. The right hand pair from A works a cloth stitch with the passive from C. The right hand pair from B works two cloth stitches through the top passive pairs. It is necessary to twist pairs from B and C before use.

At C the footside pairs hang to the right of the pin, and the inner pair works two cloth stitches through the passive pairs to pin d. At pin B two pairs hang to the left of the pin; the inner pair works two cloth stitches through the passives to pin d. The pairs meeting at d work a cloth stitch, one pair extra is added to work the ground, and pin d is covered with cloth stitch. These two pairs become footside weavers and work back to pins E or F. The footside on the vertical sides of the square is straightforward. Along the top the normal footside is worked on the outside edge. Pin g was added to prevent an unsightly space; the weaver is twisted, pin g is put up and the weaver returns to the outside edge. No pairs were added at g. At pin h two pairs are added for the ground. Pairs will be added at alternate pin holes only. Diagram 154(b) shows the use of pairs at the top left hand corner. Pin q is used twice. Pairs are used to make the ground as in pattern 21 on page 20.

To complete the square refer to diagram 154(c). The footside trail is worked from right to left. The additional two pairs which accumulate at alternate pins work a ground stitch without a pin and are taken, one pair at each pin, into the trail by the weaver. They are discarded to prevent unnecessary thickness. At the bottom left hand corner the edge and passive pairs pass through each other in cloth stitch and are tied together as explained on page 99. Diagram 154(d) shows the use of threads in the fruit. Motifs with decorative edges are usually more attractive, especially if the complete motif is used as a form of decoration.

## TO PREPARE MOTIFS WITH PATTERNED EDGES

The design should be placed in the centre of a large area of ground, and the outline drawn on the ground holes. Draw in possible decorative features on one quarter only. As far as possible make use of available holes. Photograph 155 shows an oval motif; the narrow edging on page 31 was arranged round the edge. If one quarter is worked out accurately, the same arrangement on the other three quarters ensures a symmetrical result. The pattern is worked from top to bottom; pricking 156 indicates the direction of working.

The motif in photograph 157 has the central feature taken from an old pattern and the edging added, using when possible holes in line with those in the ground. The six pin honeycomb rings are pricked exactly from the ground grid; the cloth shapes are rounded but still in line with the working diagonals. The pricking 158 indicates the working direction.

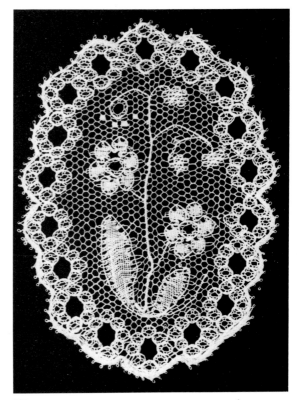

155

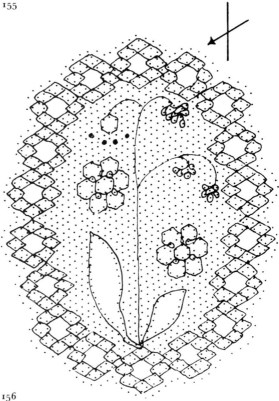

156

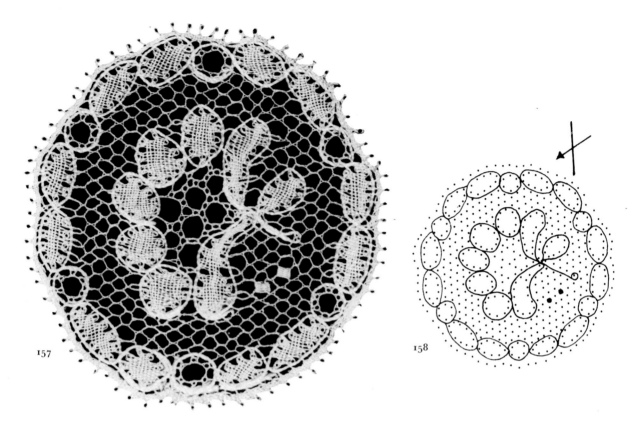

157

158

## CIRCULAR MOTIFS (SIX SECTION)

These can be planned and made very quickly; one real advantage is the small number of bobbins required for the size of the pricking. Small motifs are made using the pattern features in the narrow regular edgings. It is necessary to select a pattern that will look well at 60°. Photograph 159 shows two motifs with prickings 160. Refer to illustration 161 for the method of making the smaller motif. Take a grid at 60° and work as follows:

1. In the centre, mark in a hexagon around six holes.

2. Draw lines through opposite points and extend to the edges of the grid. This will divide the paper into six sections.

3. To plan section A, consider the line Aa as the footside and indicate the pattern *within* the section but *not* using the dividing lines. The dots surrounded by squares should not be pricked, as the outer part of the design is worked as honeycomb.

4. Turn the paper until the line Bb is in a vertical position; the pattern can be positioned in section B.

5. Turn the paper until the line Cc is in the vertical position and mark the pattern in section C.

6. Continue until the pattern is complete, and pricked onto all sections.

7. Prick the six holes within the centre ring, but do not prick the centre hole.

8. Prick the holes along the dividing lines, as well as the two holes between the cloth diamond and the honeycomb in each section.

9. Remove the grid and mark in the gimp lines as shown in the illustration.

10. Add the picot holes in one section. The ringed dot in the illustration indicate the approximate position, but without the grid a pleasing curve can be achieved.

11. Make a copy of the picot holes on clear plastic a described on page 83 and use it to complete the picots in the other sections.

### To work the motif

(Refer to illustration 161.) Position the pillow so that Aa i in a vertical position, and place an additional cover cloth or a tape along the line Aa to indicate footside position Begin the section at pin k, and complete it at pin m. Turn the pillow so that Bb is vertical and adjust the cover cloth which indicates the footside position. Work the dividing line from the head to the central hexagon; both pairs from m will work out to the picot edge. Work section B from pin n and complete it at pin o. The dividing line is worked before the pillow is turned so that the pair from the centre hexagonal ring travels back to the edge. Turn the pillow and continue until six sections are complete. A piece o clear plastic should be placed over the pin heads of the firs

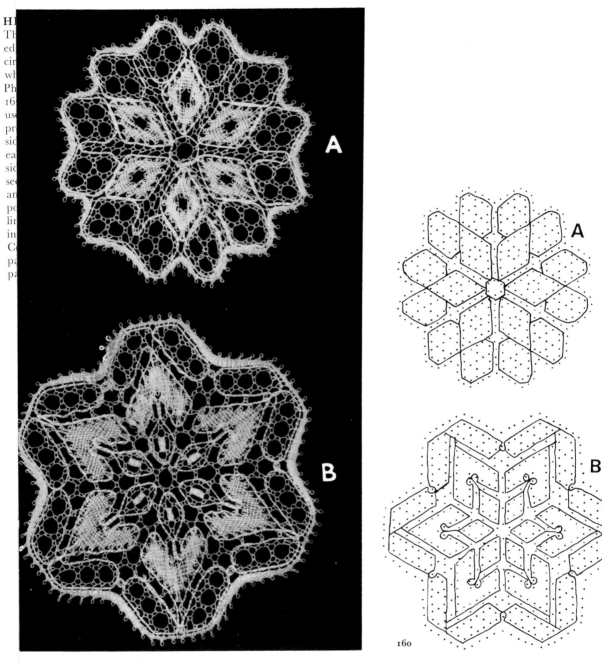

159

160

and second sections to facilitate the movement of threads when working the last sections. This is held in position by the cover cloths.

The second motif is worked similarly. However, honeycomb has been worked along the dividing lines. Alternate holes only were pricked and the 'gap' row worked; this precludes the need for a pair to travel to and from the centre hexagon.

163

## Hexagonal edgings using old floral designs

(Refer to pricking 165 and the accompanying draft pattern.) When planning a corner for an edging, as described in Chapter 4, a straight-sided mirror is placed at 45° from the footside and moved until a pleasing corner is seen. To make a hexagonal edging the mirror is placed at 60° from the footside and moved until an attractive and suitable pattern arrangement is found. Line A on the draft indicates the position. It is also necessary to find a central position to reverse the pattern, indicated by line B. Plan and prick the reversal by making two copies of the pricking between lines A and B, omit the filling between the flower and the 60° line. Scratch one copy along line B, fold the excess paper underneath and place the fold to line B on the reverse side of the other pricking. Mark in the gimp lines, adjust the new pricking and make several copies. Indicate line A at both ends of all copies. Scratch one copy along line A, fold under the excess, and match it to line A on another copy. Ascertain that the footside angle is 120°. Continue to add pricked copies until the hexagon is complete. Fasten together and prick the edging onto card and paper. Mark

in the gimp lines. Indicate the 60° lines on the paper copy and draw in the footside equivalent across the corner, at right angles to the 60° line. Select a filling for the 'corner' and add to the pricking. When satisfactory, place the copy over the card and prick through. The filling used in pricking 165 is a form of alternate honeycomb shown in photograph 166, as well as in working diagram 217 B (b).

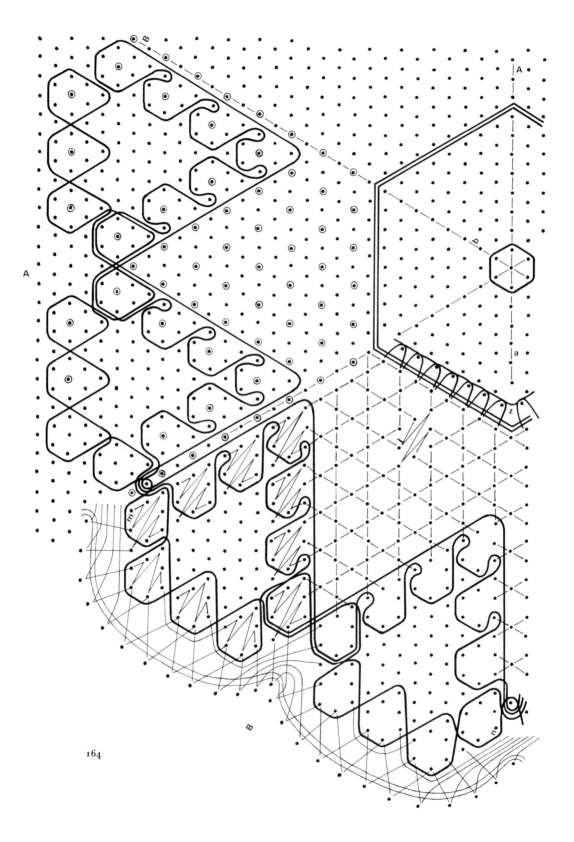

164

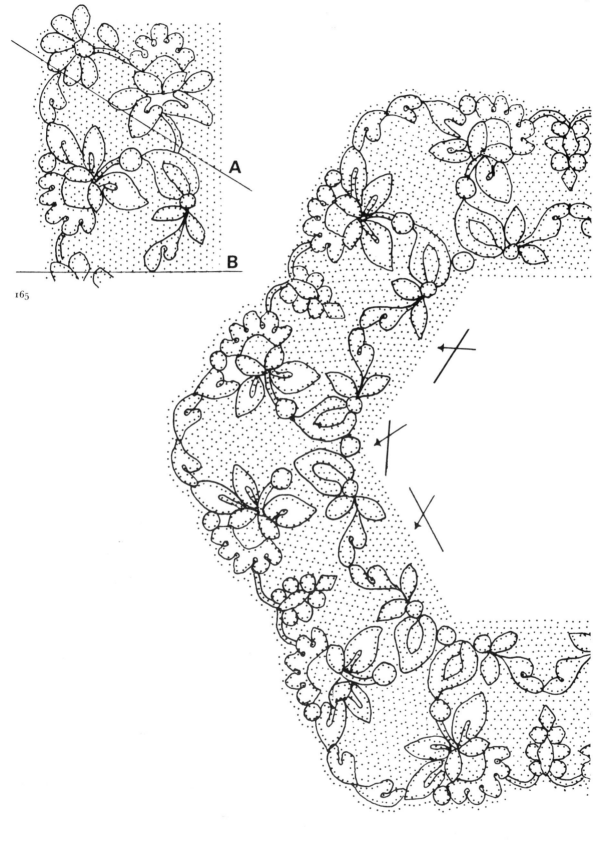

165

## ADAPTATION OF OLD DESIGNS TO MAKE SMALL MOTIFS

Some old patterns are very attractive, and a small part of the design can be copied and used elsewhere. (Refer back to photograph 157.) The use of a straight-edged mirror on drafts or prickings will often produce interesting results. Illustration 167 shows three old drafts and motifs made using this method. When making the pricking, the pattern shapes and the edge are put in and the gimp lines marked. Lastly the fillings are added using grids pricked onto transparent film. Always indicate the footside equivalent and direction of working.

*Illustration 167(a).* The centre filling is described on page 148 in diagram 223.

*Illustration 167(b).* Note the direction of working. Tallies or mayflowers may be placed in the honeycomb at the discretion of the lacemaker. If certain holes were omitted from the honeycomb pricking the filling in diagram 227 may be worked. The choice of filling depends on the effect required and the preference of the lacemaker.

*Illustration 167(c).* The fillings were added from the original draft. However, the motif can be worked using fewer bobbins if the pattern is re-pricked and the lace worked from the point of the leaf down through the centre and on to the point of the second leaf, which will lie at the bottom. The disadvantage is the difficulty of achieving a clear picot edge at the bottom when it is important to have both sides matching.

Photograph 168 and the accompanying prickings at 169 shows three more motifs made in this way. The direction of working is indicated on each pricking. The first motif was planned using the draft C in illustration 167.

## TO BEGIN LACE WITH A DECORATIVE EDGE ACROSS THE TOP

Pairs are introduced from false picots. It is important to make passive pairs cross between features, in the same way as they cross between heads on an edging. Some pairs will remain as passives but others will travel for some distance, between picots and gimp, before entering the design. The ability to work well comes with practice. However, the following suggestion may help. Before beginning to make the lace, take the paper copy of the pricking and place it with the top of the pattern to the left hand side. Visualize the arrangement of picots and passive pairs, if this was an edging, and mark the position of pairs using a pencil. Place the copy alongside the pricking on the pillow and, as far as possible, work the lace to match the copy. In most circumstances keep three passive pairs along the top; the extra pair may be used when it is not convenient to make a false picot. If necessary two pairs may be added across a gimp thread. Lay the threads one above and one under the gimp; twist on both sides to enclose it. Introduce the new pairs into adjacent pattern features or, if required, take the pair on one side out through the passive pairs to make a picot.

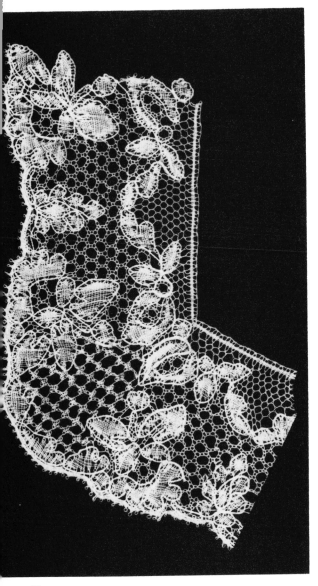

166

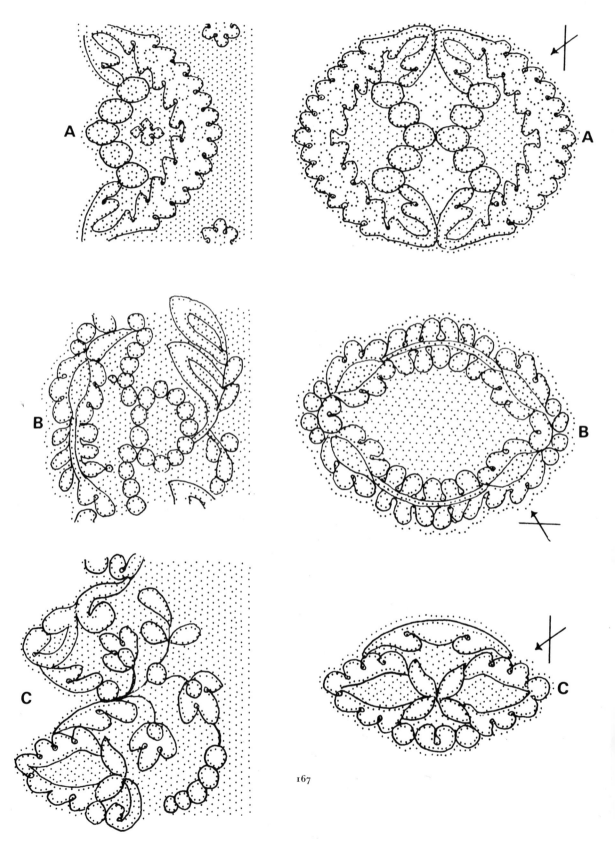

168                    169

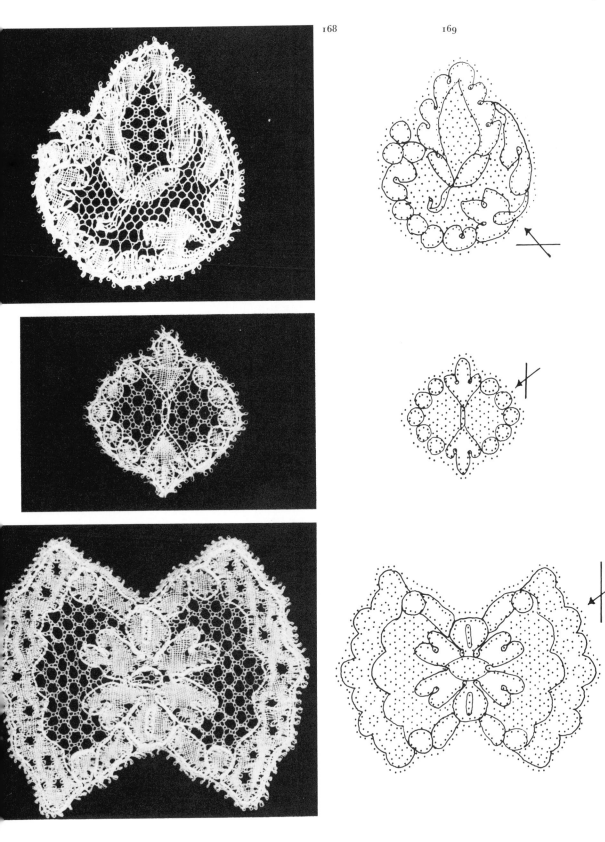

## ADAPTATION TO MAKE A FAN, COLLAR OR LARGE CIRCULAR MAT

Principles explained in this chapter and Chapter 5 must be applied. For example, it is possible to design large floral mats based on the principle of the six section motif and hexagonal edging. It is possible to use a ground or honeycomb pricking in more than one position, but once the footside equivalent has been fixed it *cannot* be altered within that area. In diagram 238 the ways in which the honeycomb can be worked have been indicated with blue diamond outlines; in each case the top pinhole (i.e. the *first* to be worked) is ringed. The footside equivalent for each way of working is indicated with a blue broken line. In the past, collars and fans were arranged to avoid the use of vast numbers of bobbins. Again, the method was to design the predominant features so that the ground was in separate sections. (Refer to diagram 170.) This method can be used today. The broken lines indicate the pattern features which must extend the full width of the fan. The footside equivalent is planned for each section independent of the others. In each case the ground will be started at the position labelled a. The divisions will be symmetrical but the number of sections will vary according to the design. The 'Carnation' fan pricking 171 is planned as shown in diagram 170. A fan pattern is too large to be accommodated readily in a book and care is needed to produce a good pricking. The 'Carnation design is shown in pricking 150 and photograph 149.

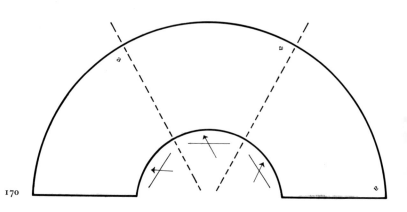

170

171

# 10 Fine Old Bucks Point Patterns

Most Bucks Point lacemakers long to work the elaborate old patterns, but too often the complexity of the pricking makes problems which bring disappointment to mar the initial enthusiasm. The cap crown, in photograph 172 and pricking 173, is a delightful pattern requiring considerable skill in interpretation and execution. Success depends on three factors, the wise choice of equipment and materials, careful pattern selection and preparation, and the knowledge to make the lace.

## PILLOW

The experienced lacemaker will have preference for a particular pillow and bobbins; however, the pillow may be unsuitable for a large piece of work. An unsatisfactory pillow may affect the tension and method and perhaps result in unfinished work. Too often, people use very large, flat pillows for the making of fans and large collars. Initially it will appear to be advantageous to have the pricking displayed in this way, but as work progresses the problems become irritating and eventually insurmountable.

If the work is started at one side of the pillow, large numbers of bobbins may fall over the edge and require much sorting out each time they are used. Threads will break if the pillow is moved and the bobbins disturbed. If the pillow has a big flat area the lace may rise up the pins, and if the pillow is domed the pricking will not lie close to the pillow at the 'corners'. Pins may not enter the pillow and the tension becomes poor. To avoid confusion bobbins are sometimes layered with cloths between, which in turn creates difficulties as the threads are worked in the air and the stitches will not lie at the base of the pin. Furthermore, any large pillow necessitates the lacemaker working in an uncomfortable position; neck ache or back ache may result and sometimes the only way to use such a pillow is to stand in order to manipulate bobbins and pins.

A good old-fashioned bolster pillow will solve many problems provided that it has a diameter of 500mm (20in). The pricking will fit the pillow closely, and the bobbins may fall all round or be supported in groups by large pins. If the bolster is big enough there will be a large flat area on top, so that the working area is very like that on the flat pillow so popular today. The choice of fabric for pillow and cloths is important. These patterns require many hours of work and it is more restful to have a plain colour. It is preferable to use green, blue or another dark colour (other than black) rather than flowers, stripes or spots which can

cause headache and eye strain. If the pillow has to be moved, a sheet of foam rubber or plastic 10mm ($\frac{1}{2}$in) thick can be placed over the bobbins to keep them in order and prevent thread breakage.

## THREAD

In the past fine cotton and linen were used, but gradually the need for these threads declined and now they are no longer available. The thread should be two or three cord twisted and able to withstand laundering and storage. Linen thread would be ideal but the 140/2 produced in Belgium is suitable only for the coarser patterns. Thread manufactured for a variety of purposes other than lace is used.

Retors D'Alsace and Brilliante D'Alsace threads made by Dolfus Meig et Cie are intended for machine embroidery but they work up very well for Bucks Point lace. It is a soft thread with which good tension can be maintained, but the finished lace lacks the crisp finish so much admired in the past.

Unity 150 is manufactured by the English Sewing Company. It is a glace thread and works up well with a good firm ground. As the thread is smooth and fine it can be used on some of the fine old prickings. Normally it is sold on 10,000-metre cops (about 11,000 yards) but D.J. Hornsby and Audrey Sells sell it in small quantities.

Pearl cotton is available in sizes 5, 8 and 12. No. 5 is too thick for Bucks Point lace but 8 and 12 are used as gimp threads. It is necessary to have a soft thread that is not highly twisted. No. 12 is used with the Retors D'Alsace nos. 50 and 60 also with the Unity 150. No. 8 is used with Retors D'Alsace no. 40 on the coarser pricking where the holes are 2mm ($\frac{1}{12}$in) apart on the footside. Occasionally the no. 8 pearl cotton is used with the finer thread depending on the effect required. Black lace can be made using the Retors D'Alsace thread and pearl cotton. D.M.C. Retors D'Alsace and pearl cotton is available in black, ecru or white.

## PATTERNS

In order to choose a pattern, one must either have seen the lace or be able to interpret the pricking. In the beginning it is preferable to select a small motif or a fairly narrow edging. Practice is necessary to get good results and it is better to wait until one is adept at handling a pillow with a large number of bobbins and has had ample opportunity

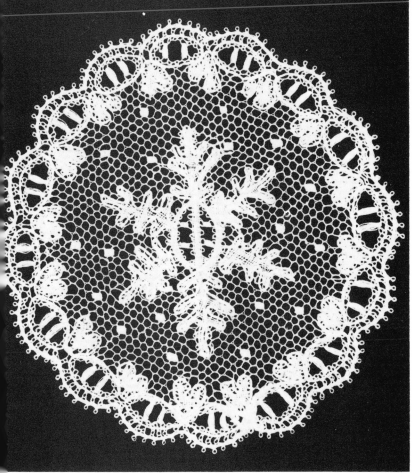

172

to work leaves, scrolls and flowers before beginning the fan or collar that will take many months to complete. Many old patterns are very fine and it is no longer possible to obtain thread or pins suitable; some patterns have a lot of pin chain and open spaces and were originally used for black lace. It is important to visualize the finished lace and know the purpose for which it is intended.

Chapter 6 discusses the pricking of patterns and the need for accuracy. The pricking must be good and clearly marked in black ink. It takes many hours to prepare a pricking; the impatient lacemaker will paste a photocopy onto card and perhaps give it a colour wash. To achieve a good pricking the pattern must be pricked on a flat surface, therefore the whole must be pricked before it is placed on the pillow. If difficulty is experienced when the gimp lines are added, the method described earlier in this book can be used. The pattern features are pricked first, the copy removed and the gimp lines inked onto the card. The copy is replaced exactly and the fillings and ground are added afterwards. Another difficulty that arises when pins are put into a photocopy is that they rarely obliterate the black dot. When ground is undone because of an error, it is almost impossible to count and check the holes, as holes and dots cannot be analysed. When patterns are pricked, always make a paper copy which can be used for reference. The position of pairs in honeycomb or other filling, the path of the weaver in a cloth scroll or the use of pairs for picots may be drawn on the paper copy to facilitate working.

173

## SKILLS

The understanding and working of patterns comes from experience. All lacemakers should begin with a few regular patterns, edgings and insertions. If corners are worked, this is an excellent introduction to the less regular pattern. At the corner pairs are used as available and others are added as required for appearance and strength. The working of hexagons and bookmarks gives ways of adding pairs and reducing the number when they are no longer needed. The lacemaker who becomes obsessed with the need for every pair to move in a regular geometric pattern has worked too many geometric patterns or fails to appreciate the delight of the floral laces. A thorough scrutiny of old lace will give insight into methods used in the past when lacemaking was a means of livelihood and it was important to work quickly.

Today the lacemaker is making lace for pleasure and she seeks perfection. Some of the lace made at the present time is probably more accurate than ever before, and whilst one delights in the standards achieved, it must be remembered that minor imperfections are rarely noticed and worry only the lacemaker who examines her work very closely. The desire for perfection must be balanced against common sense and a wise use of time. If one is able to study the Lace Dealer's sample book it is reassuring to see lace worked from similar prickings that has been interpreted quite differently, and sometimes there is different interpretation within the same piece of lace; the latter is obviously an error. If the lace looks attractive and the ground and fillings are accurate, it may be foolish to undo lace as the threads unravel and are weakened. The chief difficulties are to marry the curves of the flowing designs with the regular ground and geometrically based filling stitches, and to persuade the gimp threads to outline closely the pattern features.

A sound knowledge of the basic techniques of Bucks Point lace is necessary and this should be coupled with a willingness to experiment and apply knowledge to less regular situations. The footside, ground, use of pin holes within fillings and the need for passive pairs to cross each other to fill the gap between repeats on the headside leave no opportunity for novel ideas; there is an accepted method and result. This is emphasised in the early chapters. Many situations arise where particular care is needed with gimp threads, especially nook pins. These are explained in Chapter 3. Rules are made to help a beginner to learn the basic principles. It is necessary to create a definite method to speed up the learning process, but there are exceptions to many rules.

There should be two passive pairs on the footside, a minimum of two passive pairs at any time on the headside, and the passive cloth pairs within the pattern features should fall vertically. The first two rules are never broken, but when working an oval shape or a circle the passive pairs often fall parallel to the edge and the weaver moves on the radius. The shape of pattern features and the position of nook pins may necessitate a particular way of working. Holes forming between the ground and the pattern may spoil the appearance, but if care is taken to make the pairs enter and leave the ground on the correct

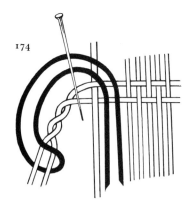

174

diagonal line the holes will be minimised. Furthermore, additional stitches without pin holes, as used in the pattern on page 50, will improve the finished lace.

Extra pairs are often needed and the addition and consequent removal of these must be executed efficiently with thought given to strength and appearance. Pairs can be added in one of the following ways:

1. Using false picots. (Refer to pages 20 and 98.)
2. Over the weaver. (Refer to diagram 174.) At the end of a row of cloth or half stitch the weaver is twisted as usual, the new pair is brought up and over the weaver and allowed to fall inside one thread. The tension on the weaver holds it in position, and this is more satisfactory than hanging the new pair on the gimp, which is so easily dragged out of position.
3. Two pairs added across the gimp thread. (Refer to page 117.) As the pairs are used both sides of the gimp thread there is no distortion.
4. Passive pairs at the beginning of a motif. (Refer to page 100.).

Pairs can be discarded in one of the following ways:

1. Discarded from cloth stitch. Refer to pages 60 and 99.) If adjacent threads from different pairs are laid back, their removal is less obvious than discarding threads from the same pair. Pairs *cannot* be removed from half stitch in this way. This method can be used in any cloth feature, for example a scroll or flower, as well as in the passive pairs on the headside.
2. Carried with the gimp thread. (Refer to pages 29 and 46.) Care must be taken to ensure that the pairs are taken as far as possible in the direction in which they were travelling. The method is not ideal, but in a fine pattern the pairs can be held close to the gimp thread and are almost invisible.

Knots can be avoided in one of the following ways:

1. When a knot appears on a thread in an area of cloth stitch, take the bobbin with the knotted thread and twist it with the adjacent thread. Take the knotted thread back and loop it round a pin placed to the side of the pricking so that the knot remains behind the work. Bring the thread back, twist it with the adjacent thread and continue work normally. The closeness of the cloth holds the thread in position. This method is used in cloth stitch only. If the weaver thread has the knot, exchange it with the passive thread in one row and then discard it from the passive in the next.

2. Elsewhere take another wound bobbin and support it on a pin behind the work. Bring it alongside the thread with the knot, fasten the bobbins together and work the double thread as one for a short distance. Discard the knotted thread and continue normally. Later the ends are cut close to the lace; the threads are worked in and will not unravel.

Most of the patterns in this last section are complicated. There are several ways of using the threads to achieve the desired effect; however, each pattern is accompanied by hints and references to earlier patterns to help the lacemaker obtain satisfactory results. Without doubt honeycomb is the most popular filling, but several of the old fillings are included, each with a working diagram.

1. This pattern, photograph 175, may have been worked originally in black thread; it is unusual to see a broad pattern with so little kat stitch. It is very likely that the draft would have been re-pricked onto the left (head) side of a strip of kat stitch ground to make a wider edging. The pattern features may have been worked in half stitch; the cloth stitch effect is rather solid when using black thread. The pricking is made from the draft pricking 176.

**175**

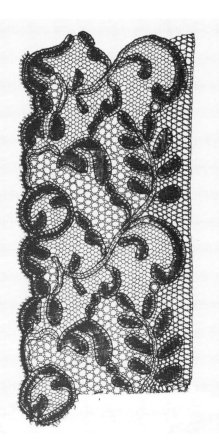

**176**

2. Typical of black lace this pattern, photograph 177, has the coarse kat stitch ground and point ground used as a filling. The solid features are worked in half stitch, and pin chain with mayflowers is an attractive filling. Working diagram 178 gives instruction for the working of pin chain fillings. Usually they are pricked on a finer grid than that used for the point ground, so that the holes are very close together. When preparing a pricking on clear plastic, it is easier first to prick the holes where the lines cross each other, i.e. the points of the diamonds, and then to add the

two pin holes between each afterwards. It is necessary to use a ruler to keep the lines straight. Mayflower can be worked in cloth or half stitch. Referring to the working diagram note that the weaver travels to a and back to b, but no pairs are available to join the cloth stitch. Similarly at c and d, no pairs are left out; because the pins are close together and the weaver is well twisted round the pin the effect is pleasant and decorative. The mayflowers will be arranged as shown in the pricking 179. The pin chain between the mayflower is worked as shown by the arrows

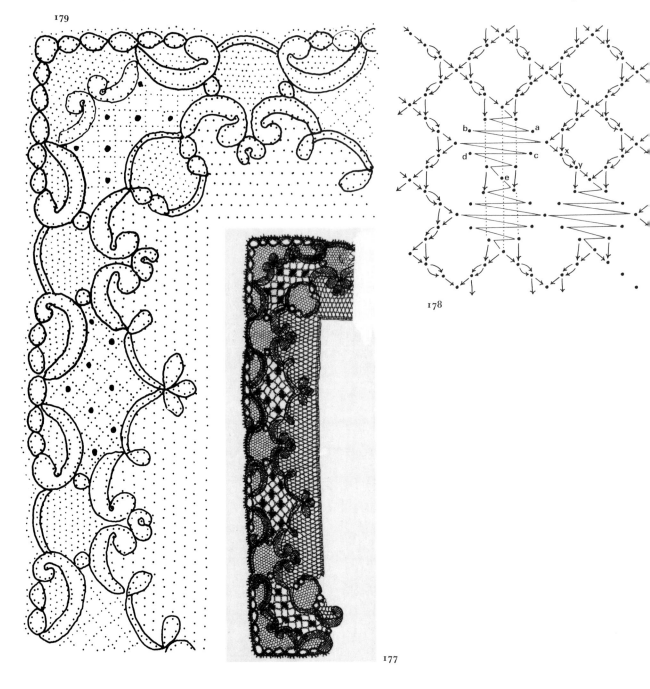

179

178

177

in the diagram. Honeycomb stitch is worked before pin x is put in position, pin x is enclosed with a honeycomb stitch and immediately pin y is put up and enclosed by a honeycomb stitch. There is only one stitch between the pins x and y.

3. This insertion uses the same pin chain pricking as the previous pattern. The mayflowers are arranged differently. (Refer to photograph 180 and pricking 181.) The working diagram 178 illustrates the working of a line of mayflowers. The cloth stitch which encloses pin e begins the next mayflower, the right hand pair is the weaver which immediately picks up the pair falling from the previous mayflower. The position of the mayflowers can create very different effects as shown in these patterns.

180

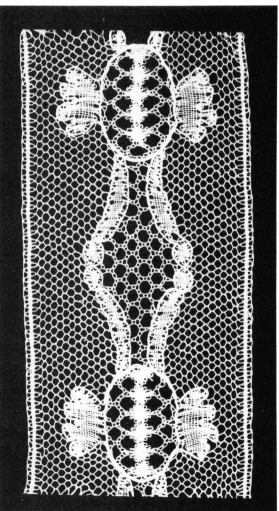

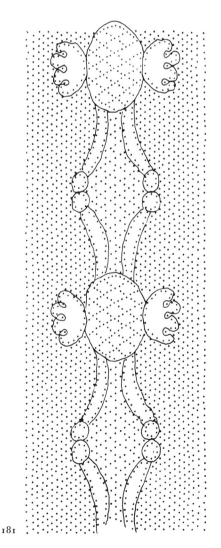

181

4. Known as the Grecian this pattern, photograph 182 was a favourite in Downton, near Salisbury; the pricking, 183, is also to be found in the collection at Luton Museum. Worked at an angle of 52°, the nine half stitch diamonds in the ground add an interesting and unusual feature. The pattern on page 71 has cloth diamonds in the ground; these patterns are excellent as continuous edgings but do not make attractive corners. One pair of gimp threads is required; the use of the gimp is shown in diagram 184.

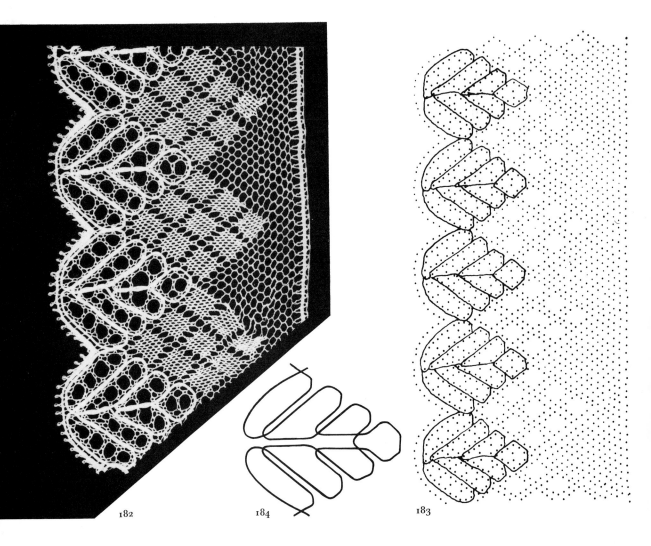

182                    184                    183

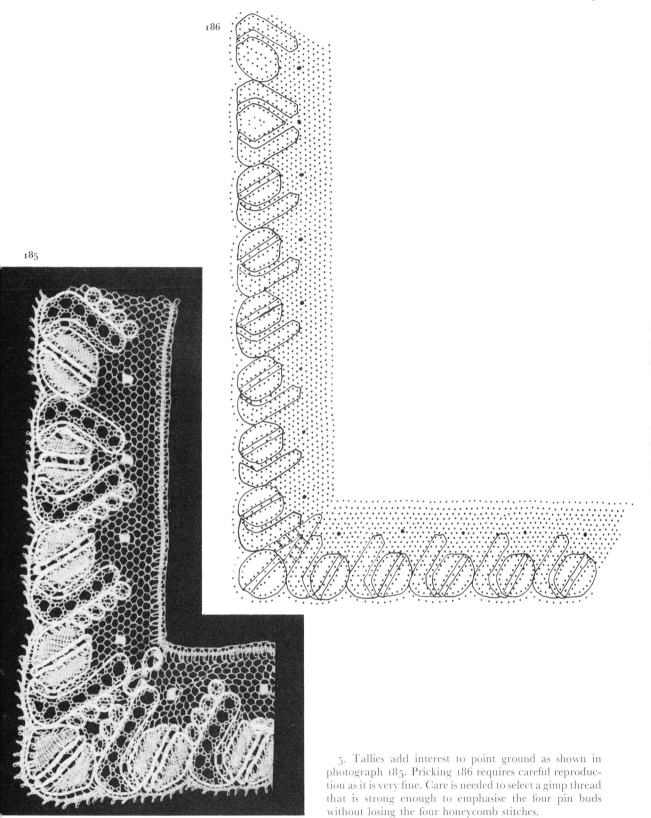

185

186

5. Tallies add interest to point ground as shown in photograph 185. Pricking 186 requires careful reproduction as it is very fine. Care is needed to select a gimp thread that is strong enough to emphasise the four pin buds without losing the four honeycomb stitches.

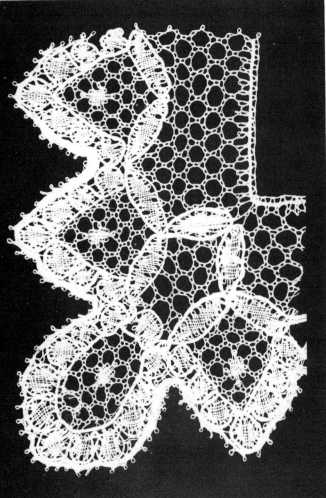

187

7. Honeycomb rings with and without tallies are found in the delightful old pattern, photograph 189, with pricking 190. The honeycomb rings with a strong gimp thread are sufficient to outline the area of honeycomb and separate it from the ground. However, on the headside the four rings require tallies to maintain the firm outline to the pattern. Often old prickings have indistinct markings and the use of tallies within rings may enhance a piece of lace. Tallies are used in this way on page 106.

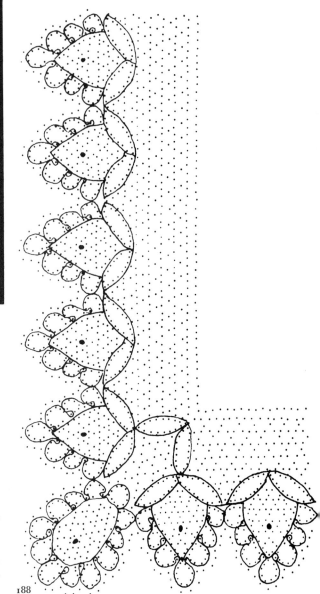

6. Photograph 187 shows lace with ground and filling in honeycomb stitch. However, the finer grid used for the filling and the central mayflower creates a different effect. (The working of mayflowers in ordinary honeycomb is described on page 22.) Two pairs of gimp threads are required, one pair to work the pointed headside and the other for the oval shapes. On the headside the outer gimp thread works nook pins to give the impression of gimp surrounding cloth buds, and the inner gimp thread remains close to the continuous row of honeycomb. The pattern on page 164 is worked similarly. In the first half of the head the outer gimp surrounds the last pin in each cloth bud and in the second half of the head it surrounds the first pin in each cloth bud. The lace is worked from pricking 188. Note that the honeycomb is pricked across the corner in the two areas enclosed by cloth features.

188

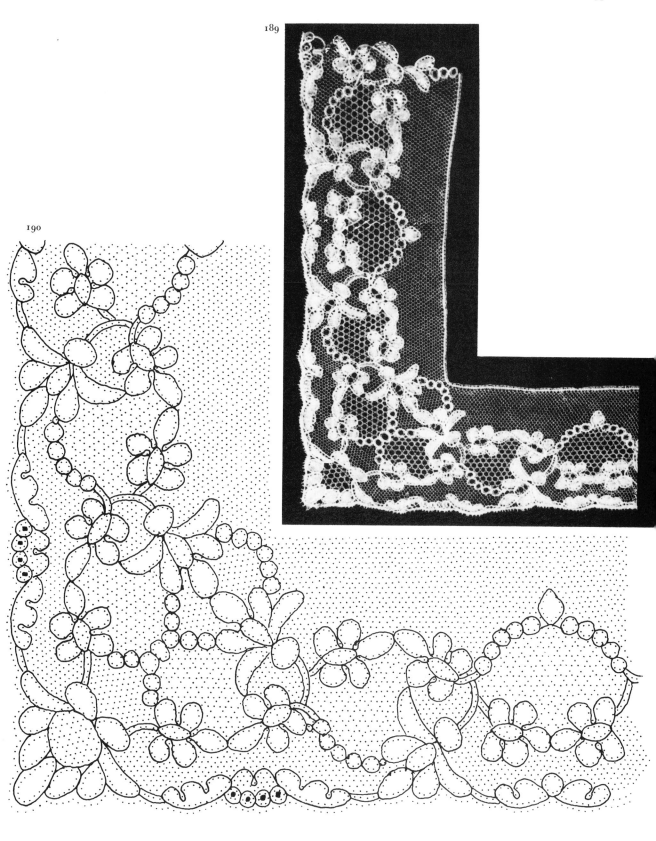

189

190

8. The small piece of lace in photograph 191 was worked from pricking 192. It shows the use of tallies to take threads across a large honeycomb edged ring. At the beginning of the pattern repeat the ground provides the pairs for the honeycomb stitches and the tallies. It can be seen in the photograph that the pairs pass round the gimp between rings and are transferred across each ring by tallies until they re-enter the ground at the end of the repeat. This principle is used in black lace as it gives a light, open effect. When making the lace the lacemaker must decide which six pinholes will provide pairs for tallies before starting the ring. The first pinhole to be worked will be to one side of the six holes, as the pairs from the first pin run in each direction to make a continuous edge to the ring.

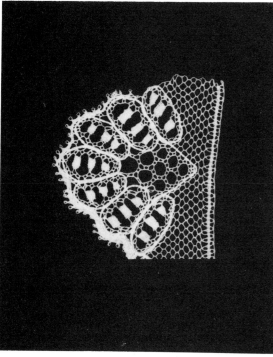

191

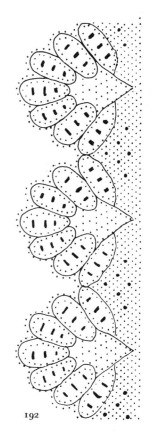

192

9. The edging in photograph 193 was worked in the
East Midlands and in Downton, where it was known as
Princess. The corner is a recent addition. The mayflowers
echo the design in the edging and the flower provides
interest in a large area of honeycomb that is difficult to
avoid. One pair of gimp threads outline the petals, one
thread travelling in each direction. Another pair works the
centre ring. The tally adds depth to middle of the flower;
there are insufficient pairs to work it in any other way. This
pattern is easily adapted to make an attractive insertion.
(Refer to pricking 194.) Draw a line through the top and
bottom pinholes of the centre honeycomb rings. Prick the
holes on the line and every hole to the left of them. Make a
paper copy at the same time and use this to position the
holes on the right hand side of the insertion. The centre line
of holes is common to both; use a straight edge to complete
the pricking and line it up with the holes pricked on the left
hand side. Diagram 238 shows the honeycomb and
mayflowers.

194

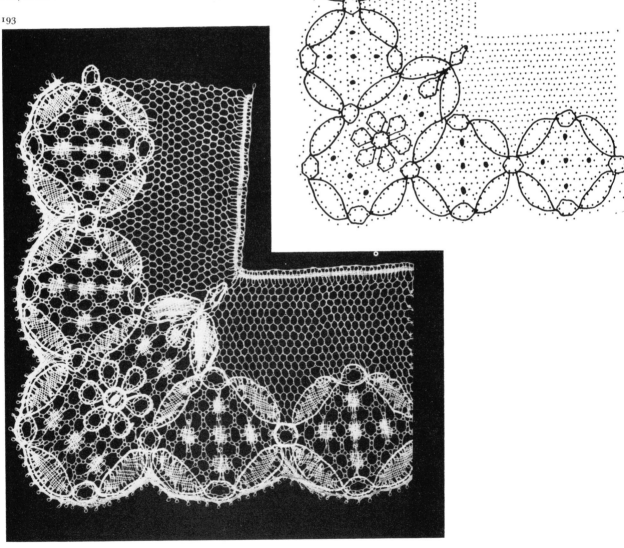

193

195

196

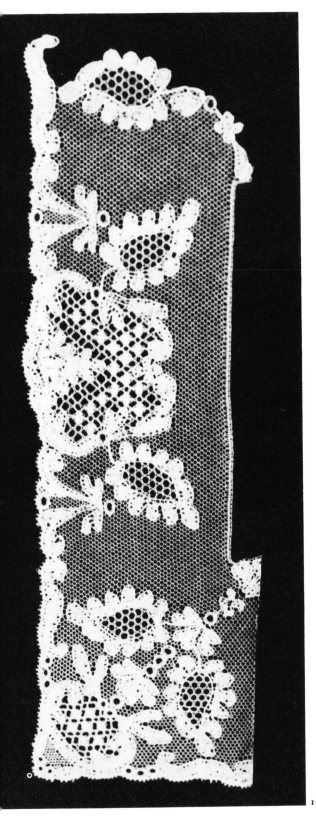

10. One of the most attractive fillings is the old may-flower found in the North Bucks Lace Association pattern known as the 'oak leaf'. The cost of the handkerchief in 1900 was £1 10s. (£1.50) as illustrated in the catalogue (photograph 195). The pricking, 196, has been taken from a N.B.L.A. parchment and requires careful reproduction. Photograph 197 shows detail to assist in the working of the lace. Diagram 198 explains the method of working the old mayflower filling. The weaver is twisted three times as it passes round pins a and b as no pairs are available to be brought in at these pins. Similarly, at pins c and d pairs are not discarded after the pins. The small loops which appear when the pins are removed and the large cloth diamonds separated by the circles of honeycomb make this very different from the simple honeycomb used in so many patterns. The cloth feature which extends beyond the normal footside in the corner will require extra bobbins and is worked diagonally. Two passive footside pairs should be retained and the normal footside worked.

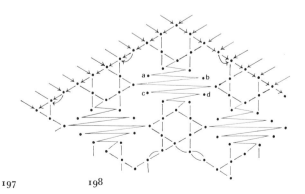

197                 198

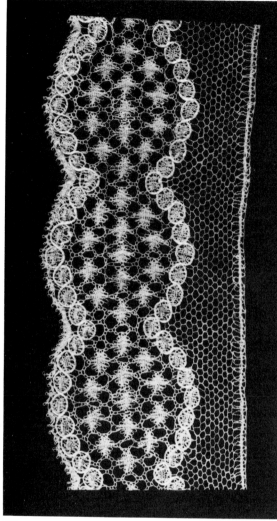

199

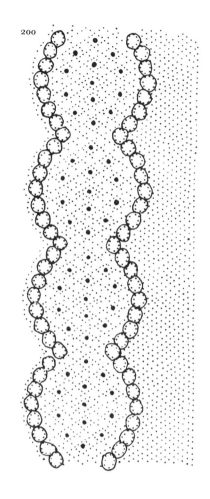

200

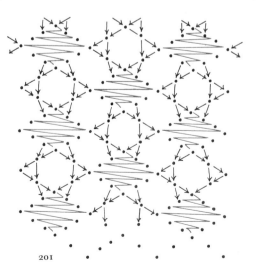

201

11. This pattern (photograph 199), pricked from an old parchment, shows a variation of the old mayflower filling. (Refer to the pricking 200.) Many of the older patterns have a different arrangement of holes and the filling has a closer, more solid effect. Diagram 201 illustrates the filling. The cloth diamond with four holes on each side is fitted into a three hole position. The pricking is made as for the simple mayflower on page 154 but the centre hole on each side of the mayflower is omitted and two holes put in close together. In diagram 201 the mayflowers are spaced regularly, but in the lace pricking 200 the mayflowers have been arranged to follow the curve of the design. To accommodate this arrangement the centre mayflower in each repeat is surrounded by pin chain. It is only by studying prickings and lace that one can begin to see some of the many ways in which the designers of the past created such delightful patterns. The filling is easy to work provided that the lacemaker understands the importance of the diagonal lines and the need to work them to feed pairs into the cloth diamonds. The small cloth rings emphasise the curve of the design.

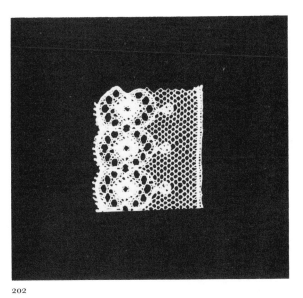

202

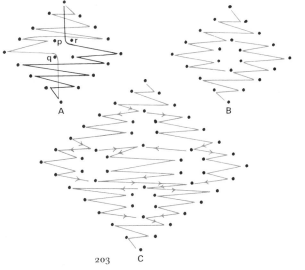

203

12. Photograph 202 illustrates the lace for pricking 120. The hexagonal shape is surrounded by honeycomb and should be filled with cloth broken by a four pin hole. The instruction for working this is given in diagram 203(a). The hexagon is considered as a diamond as the weaver goes out round the gimp at the point to achieve a close piece of cloth. Therefore the weaver works the last side pin of the hexagon and travels back through the three pairs towards the centre, but not through the centre pair. Pin p is put up to the left of the weaver, which travels to the left, round the gimp to work the honeycomb and back through the same three pairs as previously. Pin q is put up to the left of the weaver, which is hanging ready to become a passive pair in the cloth. Pin r is put up to the right of the centre passive pair; it becomes the new weaver and continues as shown in the diagram. Prickings should be studied carefully as many lacemakers will always use this arrangement to work honeycomb with a tally in the centre; in some instances this may be preferable, but sometimes it is advantageous to adopt the hole in cloth to add weight to a design.

13. Six pin holes in cloth are more common than four pin holes. Photograph 204 shows the cloth diamond with the six pin hole and diagram 203(b) illustrates the method of working. The use of weavers to achieve the hole can be worked out logically and easily if a paper copy of the pricking has been made. Holes exist in less regular shapes, for example leaves, and may be worked by using the same principle. In the lace shown here the hole in the centre of the cloth circle has eight holes; this is shown in the pricking 205.

14. Occasionally several holes appear in one area of cloth; they may be geometrically arranged as in the lace, photograph 206, or as required in a less regular shape. Pricking 207 shows the position of the diamond within honeycomb and diagram 203(c) illustrates the method of working. It cannot be overemphasised that the working of holes has to be planned for each hole in its own situation and that a diagram can give only the general principle to be followed. It is interesting to see the difference between this and the previous pattern, the former with cloth rings on the headside and the latter with six pin honeycomb rings. A new pair of gimp threads is introduced for each bell shape and discarded at its completion.

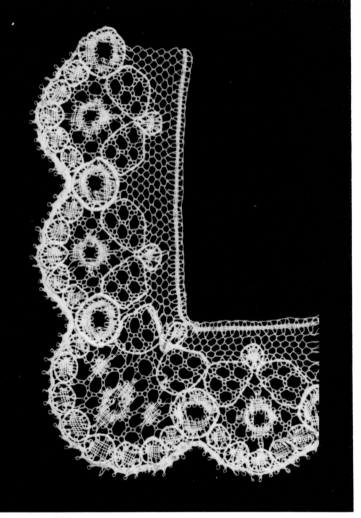

204

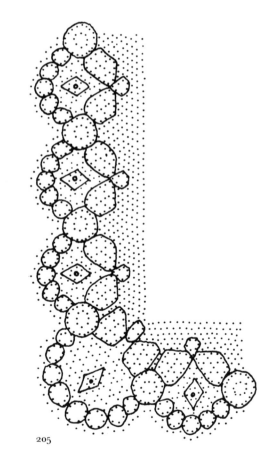

205

15. A very solid filling which gives the appearance of holes within cloth is shown in the lace in photograph 208 and pricking 209. The filling looks more attractive when seen at a distance; the cloth and open rings add to its charm. A simple pattern of this type can be interpreted in a variety of ways, but the original was worked in this way.

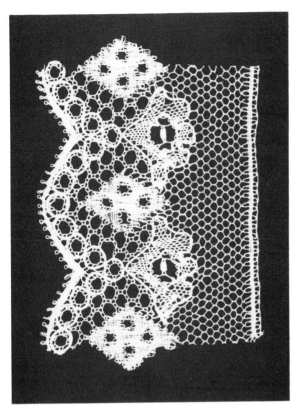

206

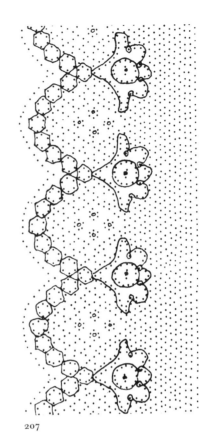

207

208

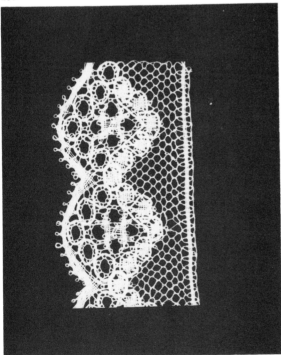

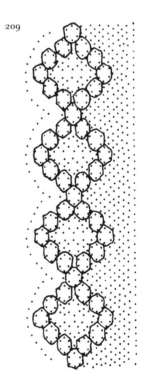

209

16. Lace depends on the complete design for its beauty. However, in some patterns the variety and continuity of the features are important, whilst in others interest is focussed on the fillings. This edging in photograph 210 depends upon the interesting shapes and flowing design; the honeycomb filling lacks decoration and provides a background. The honeycomb must be perfect and display accuracy and continuity into the small areas between the pattern shapes. It should not distract the eye from the design. It can be worked fairly quickly from pricking 211.

17. The interest in the design in the lace in photograph 212 depends on the pattern shapes. The pricking 213 shows each repeat with its cloth diamond extending into the ground. The area of honeycomb is small, but clear and well positioned, to give two vertical rows of complete rings. The centre reversal is very attractive. As an alternative the pattern could be pricked with three reversals on each side, in which case the corner would remain in the correct position and require no adjustment.

211

210

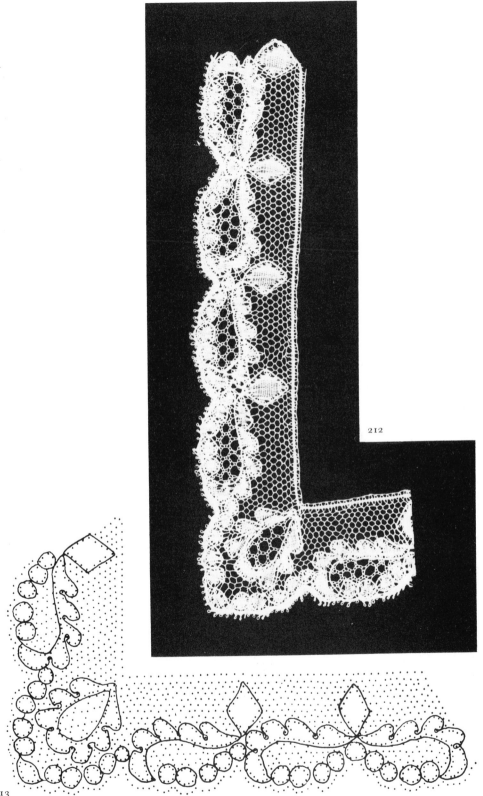

212

213

18. Lords and Ladies is a pattern (photograph 214)
with two simple but interesting fillings. The pricking 215
needs care to get the mayflowers and the tallies marked in
the correct position. Mayflowers are explained on page 22
and diagram 216 illustrates the working of the vertical bars
of cloth and the tallies made by the weavers. Holes in cloth
have been discussed earlier in this chapter; in this pattern
the weavers work tallies across the holes for extra interest.
The weaver in the cloth features near the headside travels
out to work the picots as described on page 38. On the
inside it passes round the gimp and the pin is put up
between gimp thread and weaver. The weaver is twisted to
give a neat, corded effect around the pin. At the end of each
honeycomb and mayflower filling a pair of gimp threads
has to be discarded. A fresh pair is added to surround the
filling of vertical cloth bars and tallies. In this type of
pattern gimp threads are used, added and discarded as
required to achieve the most pleasing result.

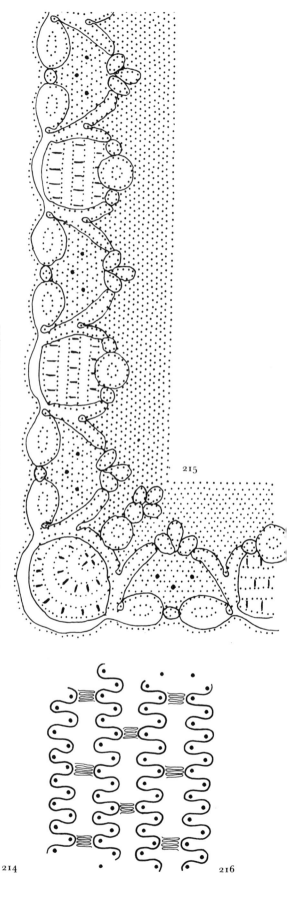

215

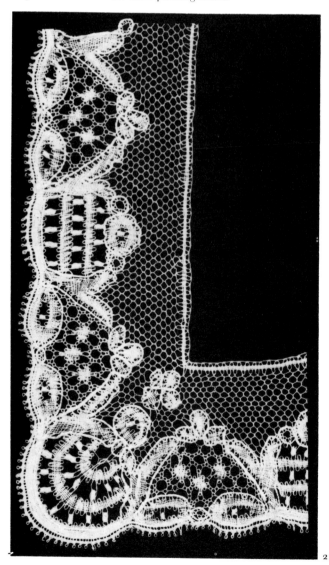

214

216

19. The prickings for another filling, alternate honeycomb, are shown in diagrams 217(a) and (b). The emphasis when pricking or making the lace is on the continuous row, as this facilitates understanding and therefore speed in working. However, the diagonal line which appears in the finished lace runs in the other direction. This is important if a special effect is sought, or if both prickings are used to achieve a reversal, as in the lace in photograph 218. The diagonal lines in the lace appear to run from ground to cloth and from cloth back to ground. Refer to the pricking 219 and note the direction of the continuous rows. This filling is used in the square on page 105. Diagrams 217 (a) and (b) part **a**) explain this method of working. Part **b** of each diagram explains another filling using the same arrangement of holes. The filling in the pattern on page 105 is worked according to part **a** of

diagram 217(b). The Torchon type of spider is occasionally found, and is considered by many people to be one of the less successful fillings. This is because Bucks Point lace is based upon an angle greater than 45°, while the spider filling is usually pricked at the same angle as the ground and does not really appear compatible with the rest of the design. Spiders are shown in diagram 220. Each line represents one pair of bobbins. Two pairs come from each side and are passed through each other smoothly in cloth stitch. A pin is put up in the middle and the pairs are once more passed through each other. There are no twists round the pin, but between spiders each pair is twisted three times. The filling in pattern number 22 looks attractive and may be pricked instead of the spider hole arrangement.

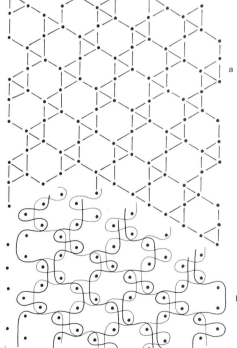

217(a)

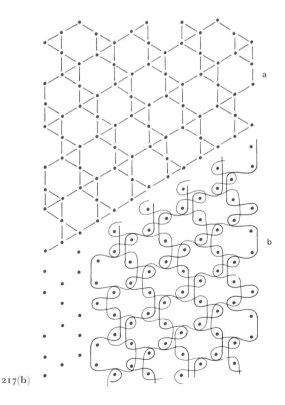

217(b)

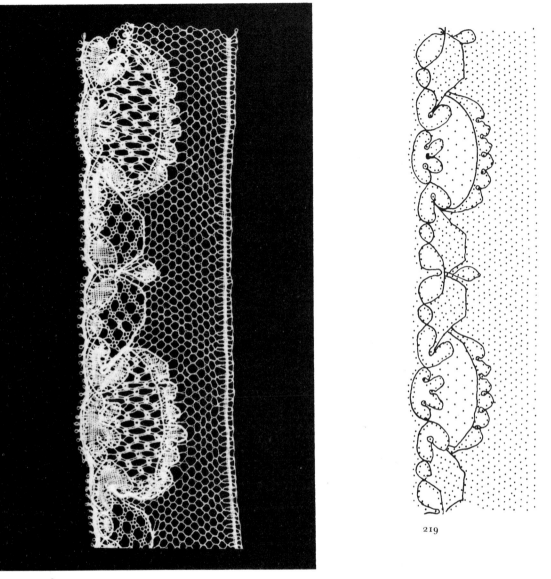

218

219

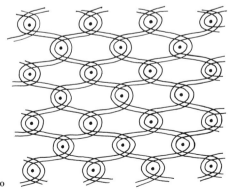

220

20. The lace in photograph 221 has another filling which at first sight shows little resemblance to the pricking. Before making the pricking 222 refer to the diagram 223. To plan the pricking on a grid, draw a line through every third diagonal row from the footside. Then draw a line through every third diagonal row towards the footside. Groups of four pin holes remain and these are required for the cloth stitch diamond shapes. Prick onto clear plastic. Scratch lines diagonally both ways through the centre of each diamond. Scratch lines as well on the diagonals that were originally omitted. The remaining holes fall on the intersections of the scratch lines, but only on those lines that fall between the cloth diamonds. It is not

an easy pricking to make, but quite straightforward if the diagram is used as a guide. If the lacemaker wishes to work the alternative filling, only the four holes to make the diamond are necessary. Work the filling following the diagram; the blue weaver denotes a small area of cloth stitch and the pin holes between are worked in honeycomb stitch. The pairs must be twisted after the cloth diamond before working the honeycomb stitch. The alternative filling is worked by taking the pairs that hang diagonally from the diamond and making a short plait, i.e. three half stitches before beginning the next cloth diamond. If the lacemaker wishes to work cloth rather than honeycomb rings extra pairs of bobbins will be required.

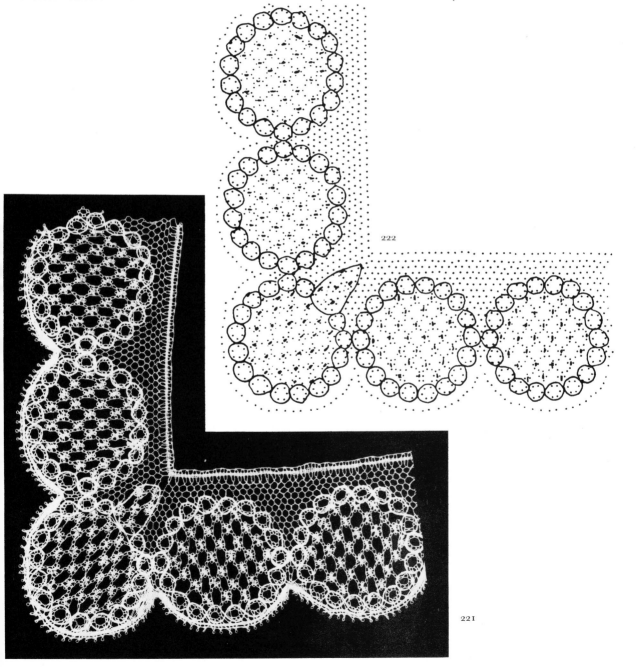

222

221

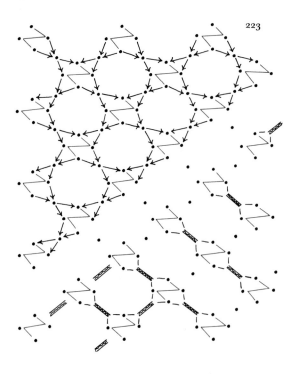

**223**

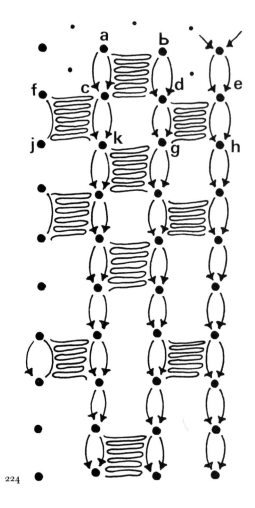

21. Vertical rows of holes may be worked in several ways, one of the more popular being pin chain with tallies as shown in diagram 224. Honeycomb stitches are made at a and b. The inner pairs make a tally to c and d. Honeycomb stitches are made at each side. As explained earlier, care should be taken to work the pair without the tally weaver first to help maintain well-shaped tallies. The inner pairs from f and c make a tally to j and k. On the other side pairs make a tally from d and e to g and h. When pairs from k and g make the next tally the vertical row has been established. Sometimes tallies are close together, or they may be spaced as shown. A combination of pin chain and honeycomb is in the filling in the wide pattern on page 154. The holes may also be used to achieve a lattice effect as shown in the lace in photograph 225. Pricking 226 shows one repeat in honeycomb stitch and the rest for this filling. Diagram 227 shows the working method; the weavers remain the same through the filling. They are twisted at the pins but no other twists are given. In each four pin cloth block there are three passive pairs. At the end of each block two pairs move to the left and one to the right; the weaver moves across to the right to keep the balance. From the last pin in one block to the first in the next, the weaver must pass through five passive pairs. (Refer to diagram 227.) Although the pattern is angular, it lends itself to a pleasing corner. However, the filling is not really suitable for small areas and should be reserved for wider patterns.

**224**

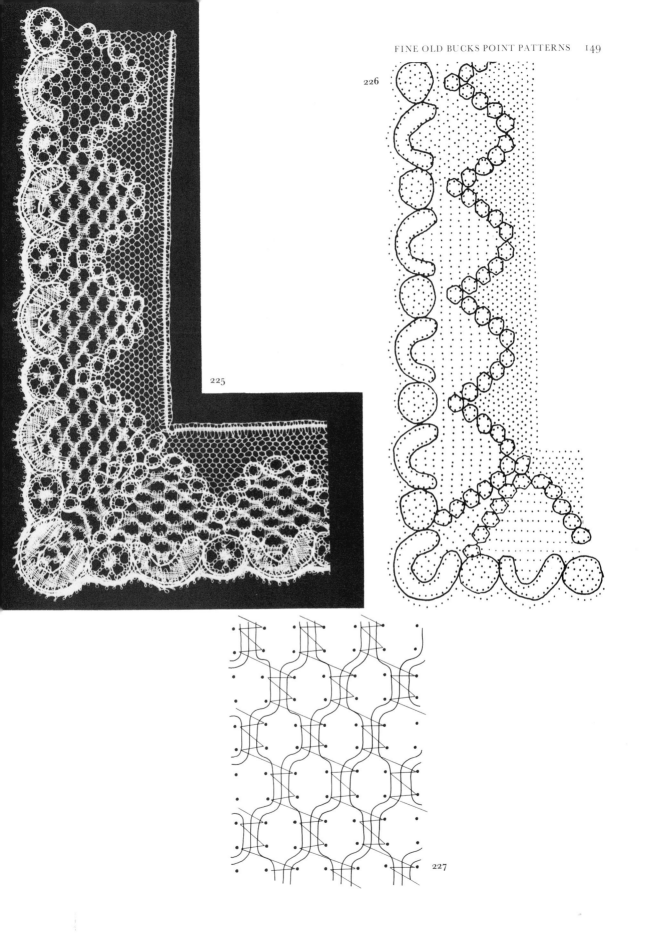

226

225

227

22.  A more definite lattice effect is the filling in the lace in photograph 228. The filling involves more work than the previous pattern. The pricking is 229 and the working diagram 230 is for the lattice section. The diagonal lines consist of two passive pairs and a weaver. The weaver must use the pins in the order shown in order to arrive at the crossing in the correct position. The weavers cross and pin a is put in position. The weavers continue through two passive pairs and pins b and c are put between the passive pairs and the weavers which are hanging outside the pins. Cross the passive pairs through each other in cloth stitch. Work the weavers each through two passive pairs to meet. Put up pin d and work the weavers together in cloth stitch. Diagram 230 clarifies the method. Between the cloth diamonds and the four pin buds is another new filling. Often it is seen covering a larger area as shown in diagram 231. To work the filling hang two pairs on each of a, b, c and d. Twist the pairs and work honeycomb stitches. It is important to remember that both pairs from the honeycomb stitch travel in the same direction. Pairs from a and b pass through each other in cloth stitch. Pairs from c and d also cross each other. Each two pairs are twisted and work honeycomb stitches at e, f, g and h. Pairs from f and g cross each other in cloth stitch, and so on. The work is most unusual in that the honeycomb stitches are made by adjacent pairs travelling in the same direction and do *not* come diagonally together.

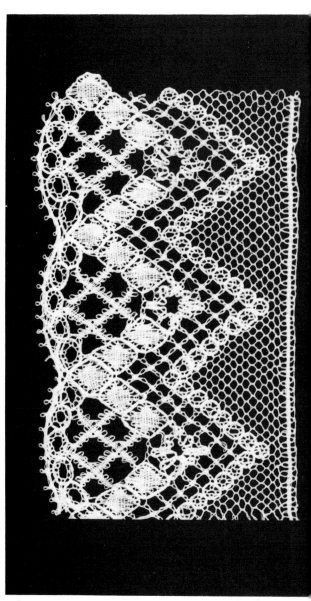

228

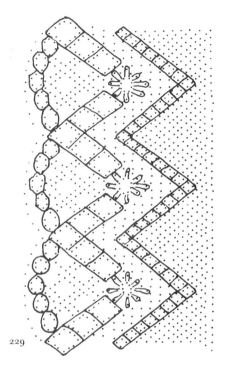

229

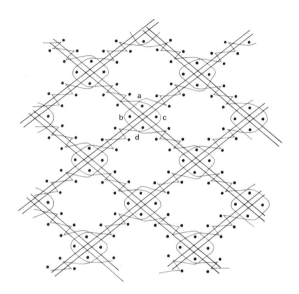

230

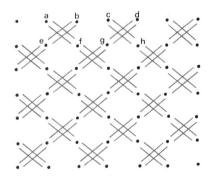

231

232

23. Photograph 232 shows lace with another filling worked in cloth stitch. The pricking is based upon the ground grid, with certain holes omitted. The lace pricking at 233 shows the arrangement clearly and diagram 234 gives the working method. The pairs which leave the corners of the cloth shapes are twisted twice, and the pairs which complete the cloth, work cloth stitch and twist to cover the pin and another cloth stitch before beginning the new cloth shape. This makes three half stitches to fill the space. This filling looks better in a large area. The same arrangement of holes is used in the filling in diagram 235, but the effect is quite different.

233

234

235

24. The Wild Briar pattern, photograph 236 and pricking 237, has a wide variety of fillings. Reference can be made to diagram 238 for the simple mayflower and later for the vertical rows of tallies within honeycomb. Diagram 216 explains the working of vertical cloth bars with tallies between. Diagram 178 shows pin chain; in this pattern it is worked without the cloth diamonds. Diagrams 198/201 illustrate the method for the old mayflower. One pattern repeat extends for 450mm (18 inches).

236

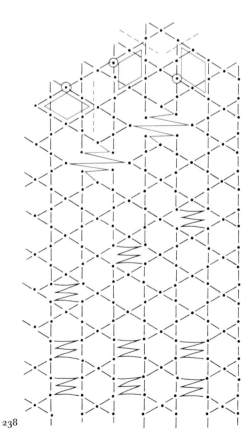

238

237

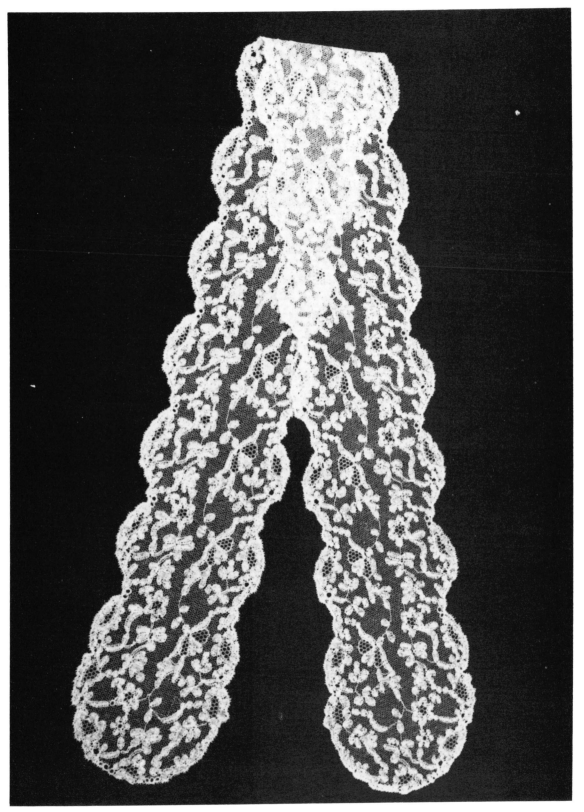

239

240

25.  The lappet in photograph 239 is 1.2m (48in) long. However, one can adjust the length when preparing the pricking 240. Photograph 241 shows detail to assist the lacemaker.

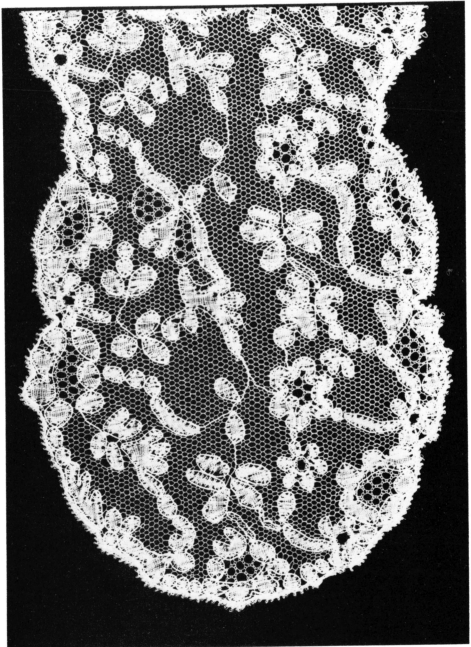

241

# Appendix

## GRIDS

These should be pricked onto parchment, transparent film or pricking card in order to have permanent copies.

A   52°   18 pin holes to each inch (25mm) on footside

B    52°    13 pin holes to each inch (25mm) on footside

C   52°   3 pin holes to each inch (25mm) on footside

D   60°   18 pin holes to each inch (25mm) on footside

60°  13 pin holes to each inch (25mm) on footside

F    60°   3 pin holes to each inch (25mm) on footside

# FILLINGS

These should be pricked onto separate pieces of transparent film or parchment and marked with footside equivalent and direction of working. Each one is based on a ground grid at 52° and 14 pinholes to each inch (25mm).

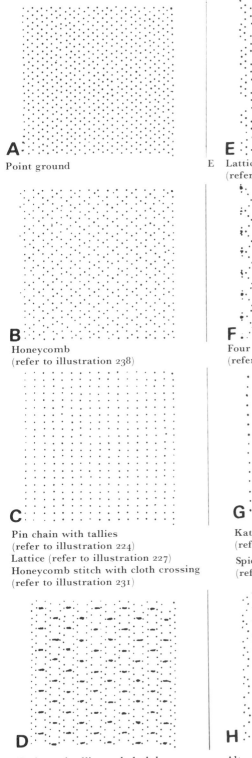

**A** Point ground

**B** Honeycomb
(refer to illustration 238)

**C** Pin chain with tallies
(refer to illustration 224)
Lattice (refer to illustration 227)
Honeycomb stitch with cloth crossing
(refer to illustration 231)

**D** Horizontal tallies and cloth bars
(refer to illustration 216)

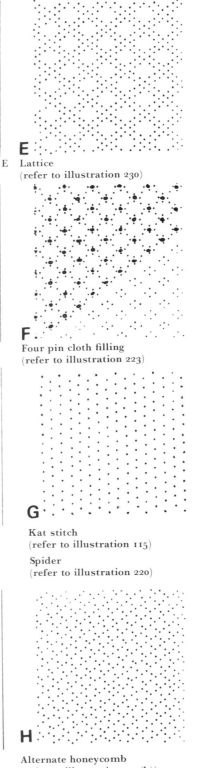

E  Lattice
(refer to illustration 230)

**F** Four pin cloth filling
(refer to illustration 223)

**G** Kat stitch
(refer to illustration 115)

Spider
(refer to illustration 220)

**H** Alternate honeycomb
(refer to illustration 217(b))

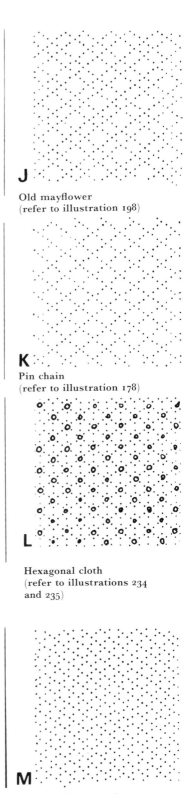

**J** Old mayflower
(refer to illustration 198)

**K** Pin chain
(refer to illustration 178)

**L** Hexagonal cloth
(refer to illustrations 234
and 235)

**M** Alternate honeycomb
(refer to illustration 217(a))

# BIBLIOGRAPHY

CHANNER, C.C., *Lacemaking, Bucks Point Ground*,
  Dryad Press, 1928.
FREEMAN, Charles, *Pillow Lace in the East Midlands*,
  Luton Museum and Art Gallery, 1958.
MAIDMENT, Margaret, *A Manual of Handmade Bobbin
  Lace*, Paul Minet, 1971.
NOTTINGHAM, Pamela, *The Technique of Bobbin Lace*,
  Batsford, 1976.
VAN HORRICK, Madeline, *Lace: our Heritage*, Joan
  Duckworth, 1980.
WRIGHT, Thomas, *The Romance of the Lace Pillow*, Paul
  Minet, 1971.

# SUPPLIERS

## UK

D.J. Hornsby
149 High Street
Burton Latimer
Kettering
Northants
(*All lacemaking requisites –
mail order service*)

Audrey Sells
49 Pedley Lane
Clifton
Shefford
Beds.
(*all lacemaking requisites –
mail order service*)

E. Braggins & Sons
26/36 Silver Street
Bedford

Mace and Nairn
89 Crane Street
Salisbury
Wilts.

T. Brown
Woodside
Greenlands Lane
Prestwood
Great Missenden
Bucks.
(*bobbin maker*)

B. Phillips
Pantglas
Cellan
Lampeter
Dyfed
(*bobbin maker*)

D.H. Shaw
47 Zamor Crescent
Thurscroft
Rotherham
S. Yorks.
(*bobbin maker*)

C. & D. Springett
251 Hillmorton Road
Rugby
Warwicks.
(*bobbin makers*)

Frank Herring & Sons
27 High West Street
Dorchester
Dorset
DT1 1UP
(*pillows, bobbins, winders*)

## USA

Berga-Ullman, Inc
P.O. Box 918
North Adams, Massachusetts 01247
*Materials and equipment*

Frederick J. Fawcett
129 South Street
Boston, Massachusetts 02130
*Large selection of linen yarns and
and threads up to size 140/2*

Osma G. Tod Studio
319 Mendoza Avenue
Coral Gables, Florida 33134
*Books, instructions, materials and
equipment*

Robin and Russ Handweavers
533 N. Adams Street
McMinnville, Oregon 97128
*Books, materials and equipment*

Lacis
2990 Adeline Street
Berkeley, California 94703
*Books, instructions, materials,
equipment and antique laces
(mail order service)*

The Unique and Art Lace Cleaners
5926 Delmar Boulevard
St. Louis, Missouri 63112
*Professional lace cleaning and
restoration*

# Index